STU
MONEY MATTERS

STUDENTS'
MONEY MATTERS

The Guide to Grants, Loans, Financial Support and Sponsorship Opportunities for Students

Gwenda Thomas

TROTMAN

This second edition published in 1994
in Great Britain by
Trotman and Company Limited
12 Hill Rise, Richmond, Surrey TW10 6UA

Students' Money Matters is developed from a major
survey conducted among students throughout the UK
by Trotman and Company Limited.
Developed from an original idea by Andrew Fiennes Trotman.

**Trotman & Company gratefully acknowledge
the sponsorship of the Midland Bank
and the Universities and Colleges Admissions Service**.

British Library Cataloguing in Publication Data

A catalogue record for this book is available from the
British Library

ISBN 0-85660-231-0

Typeset by Type Study, Scarborough, North Yorkshire
Printed and bound in Great Britain by
Biddles Limited, Guildford and King's Lynn

the
MANCHESTER
METROPOLITAN
UNIVERSITY

Meeting your future needs

with over 300 courses in 50 different subject areas...
...one of them will be right for you.

Our mission is to be an accessible institution of higher education meeting the educational and vocational needs of our students and our partners in industry, commerce and the professions.

Being Britain's largest University, we are able to offer an unparalleled choice of undergraduate, postgraduate and professional courses, most of which reflect a primary but not exclusive orientation towards some form of practical education with strong vocational links. We also have an extensive portfolio of research and consultancy activities.

Many of our courses are available in both full-time and part-time modes and a Credit Accumulation & Transfer Scheme (CATS) offers further flexibility and choice.

We have an excellent library, computing and accommodation facilities and our Students' Union offers an extensive range of sporting and recreational activities. We provide a student welfare service which can assist with accommodation, study skills development, personal and financial problems and also provides a careers advice service.

Our main location is in the centre of Manchester, a city renowned for its thriving cultural, social and sporting life. Manchester has been designated Britain's "City of Drama" for 1994 and has some of the most up to date sporting facilities in the country, including a purpose built velodrome. Some of Britain's most beautiful countryside and many other attractions and facilities lie within easy reach of the city.

The former Crewe + Alsager College of Higher Education, located in the Cheshire countryside became a faculty of the University in 1992.

For more information call our 24 hour prospectus hot-line: 061-247 1055, or write to us: The Manchester Metropolitan University, All Saints, Manchester M15 6BH.

Be a little mercenary at university.

This isn't a call for soldiers of fortune. (Money, let's face it, should never be the prime motivation for joining the Forces.)

It's the chance for school leavers, torn between university and the Army, to get the best of both worlds.

All you have to do is meet the challenge of our three-day Officer Selection Board.

Then we'll pay you a total of £25,000 to complete your course at either university or college of higher education, providing you agree to serve as an Officer for at least five years after you graduate.

That means you'll have three times as much to spend as the average student. With the promise of a demanding and exciting job once you've got your Degree.

If you only wish to commit yourself for three years, you can simply apply for a special £1,200 p.a. bursary to supplement any existing grants. But what if you're already halfway through your course?

Providing you have at least one year left to study, you can still benefit from either scheme.

For the full details, just complete the coupon below. And find out how to remain permanently at peace with your bank manager.

The Armed Forces are Equal Opportunity Employers under the terms of the Race Relations Act 1976.

There is no doubt debt problems get in the way of academic progress, and that is serious.

(Senior Assistant Registrar)

Contents

Foreword

On 30 November 1993 The Chancellor of the Exchequer, Kenneth Clarke, announced in the budget that the level of the student maintenance grant would be cut in real and actual terms. The days, weeks and months that followed the budget saw newspapers, television and radio devoting countless words to 'a skilful political budget', 'the impositions of VAT on domestic fuel costs', 'the extra tax burden on families' and so on. Little was heard of the additional financial burden to be forced on students.

All managers of companies, private and public, service and manufacturing, need their workforce to perform at the top of their ability. To do so they must be properly fed, clothed and accommodated. Students in higher education are the next generation of leaders of our society and they too must perform at the top of their ability in order to make the best of their talents.

In the next few years things will be very hard for students as financial support for them falls. This book *Students' Money Matters* is therefore very timely. It gives informed guidance on how to make the best use of students' financial resources. It is required reading for students and their parents who, if they follow its advice and use their traditional ingenuity, will cope with the challenges of a university or college career.

That Midland Bank and UCAS have joined to support this book is no gimmick. You could call it enlightened self interest. Both organisations want to see students succeed, and succeed well, in their courses for the benefit of the country as a whole. They will not do that without sound financial advice and support.

Hence the book.

Tony Higgins
Joint Chief Executive,
Universities and Colleges Admissions Service

Introduction

'When it comes to money, there is no doubt that for most UK students going on to higher education things are tough, and likely to get tougher.' This was how I introduced Students' Money Matters when first published two years ago. I was right. And now with student grants actually being cut by 10 per cent in each of the next three years, things are going to get tougher still. So unless you have parents with a bottomless purse or a private income, something has got to fill the gap in resources.

In this, the second edition of *Students' Money Matters*, we set out to investigate all the means and methods by which students can provide themselves with an income while studying for a degree, HND or other higher education qualification.

As before, we are not setting out to argue the rights and wrongs of the financial situation students find themselves in – or, in fact, to tell you what to do. The aim of *Students' Money Matters* is to give helpful information and advice; to point out the pros and cons to be considered when seeking sponsorship, loans, overdrafts, grants, work experience, industrial placements, a year out, work abroad, scholarships, etc., and to tell you how to go about getting them. It is for you to weigh up the evidence and information and make your own decisions – because what's right for you could be totally wrong for somebody else.

However, the book does include comments from employers, university tutors, careers advisers, and students. As you might expect, the undergraduates with whom we discussed *Students' Money Matters* were very forthright in their views. These have been included, uncensored. There is nothing more valuable or illuminating than a report from the battlefield!

The book also includes information on how much it is likely to cost you to 'live' as a student in different parts of the country, and advice on how to budget.

To produce *Students' Money Matters* we drew up a list of all the questions we thought you, as a student, would want to ask about financing your studies. We then set about finding the answers. As a result, the book is written largely in the form of a dialogue. The answers given have been kept as short, simple and direct as possible. We've cut through all the red tape and official jargon. Where we felt that you might want to dig deeper into a topic, alternative reference material has been suggested, along with appropriate organizations you can contact.

Occasionally you will find information has been repeated. This is to help the reader. There is nothing more irritating when you are trying to glean information quickly, than having to flick from one section to another.

Money, especially the lack of it, can be a depressing subject. We hope you'll find *Students' Money Matters* an illuminating, helpful and amusing read; and that the information given will make your studying time less worrying and a lot more fun.

When we first published *Students' Money Matters* we thought there was a need for such a publication. Now we are certain of it. And it is because of the demand that we have decided to bring out this new edition. In the first edition we asked for your comments, criticism and suggestions for the next edition. These are included here along with updated facts and figures, a new survey of the student scene and a new appraisal of the student situation. But nothing is static, least of all the pecuniary plight of students, so please keep those comments coming. It is only by being vigilant and keeping in touch with 'campus correspondents' that we can pass on the right information to those who follow.

Our thanks in helping prepare this book must go to all those students who proved an invaluable source for so much of the information; the employers, financial and higher education institutions who gave vital assistance in the research of the material.

Gwenda Thomas

Please send your thoughts, comments, anecdotes to:
Trotman & Co Ltd, 12 Hill Rise, Richmond, Surrey TW10 6UA

1
THAT'S THE WAY THE MONEY GOES

How much is it going to cost you to be a student?

. . . As much as you have, and probably a lot more. Students have always been hard up, but never more so than now.

In the last year there have been numerous stories in the press about students having to give up their degree courses because they just couldn't make ends meet. With opportunities for holiday and part-time work drying up, the situation at the moment is very bad. For some it is critical. But we do have over a million students in full time higher education in the UK at the moment, and the figure is rising. How are they managing?

There are many factors which can affect your financial situation. Some students are luckier – or perhaps more determined – than others in:

- raising additional finance;
- managing to work as well as study;
- choosing to study in cheaper parts of the country;
- living at home;
- being excellent managers.

While others . . .

- find that money slips through their fingers like water;
- are great socializers and imbibers;
- take courses which demand that they buy expensive equipment or books, or need to travel;
- have expensive tastes and hanker after all the good things of life;

- have a wide range of hobbies and interests;
- study in expensive areas such as London.

Obviously you should not pick your course where the living is cheapest, but it is as well to know what costs you are likely to face. This first chapter looks at what it is likely to cost YOU to get a degree, HND or any other higher qualification. But first . . .

What makes so many of you do it?

This year over 400,000 young people will apply for a higher education course in the UK. What is the great attraction? Why do you forefeit the chance of having money in your pocket to become a near-penniless student?

Here are some of the reasons given by students in a Heist/PCAS Survey, *Higher Education: The Student Experience**:

'There is no one in our family who hasn't got a degree.'

'Neither of my parents have been through higher education and they said you are going – FULL STOP.'

'People want graduates and you start one or two steps up the ladder.'

'I was a chef. I never had much job satisfaction. I wasn't going to be another Roux Brother.'

'I didn't want to get halfway up the management ladder and find people with degrees getting the top jobs. I wanted an exciting job at the top.'

'I was too lazy to get a job.'

'If you go into a job at 18 you will work for forty years. I wanted to put off working for as long as possible.'

'I didn't know what I wanted to do career-wise and thought I might as well keep learning until I did decide.'

'I was interested in Maths and wanted to find out more. I am disillusioned – you expect to find people in groups talking about intellectual things, but it's not like that.'

'I love studying and writing essays.'

'A stepping-stone to reality.'

* Available from Heist, The Grange, Beckett Park Campus, Leeds LS6 3QS. Price £14.95

'You get an overall development, you get an academic development and you develop socially. Your whole self changes.'

'You are experiencing more things from different angles.'

'Having been closeted in a girls' school for years, it is quite educational to be let out amongst men!'

If we asked the rest now studying in our universities and colleges across Britain, we'd probably get thousands of different answers. But whatever your reason for studying, it's going to be hard-going financially for the next few years. How are you going to manage?

YOUR FEES

Whether you are at university or college, your course fee will almost certainly be paid for by your local authority, and the actual cost will not concern you. We say 'almost certainly' because there are courses where fees are not paid, and these are covered in the next chapter. There is also a great deal of discussion going on at the moment as to whether students will be asked to contribute towards their fees in the future. As yet, the answer is NO.

YOUR LIVING EXPENSES

... are something different. You may be entitled to a maintenance grant – again, this is discussed in the next chapter – but wherever your finances come from, it's you who will have to eke them out.

ACCOMMODATION – THE MAJOR DEMAND ON YOUR FINANCES

Accommodation will probably soak up nearly half of your income. If it's full-board in university accommodation then you are looking at over three quarters of your total income.

Finding the right place to live is important, especially in your first year. It can affect your whole attitude to your college, your course, your study, the town or city where you are staying, making the right friends, and whether you actually do well. If it's half an hour's walk, or a bus ride across town, to get to the library, you may think twice about going there. If you're stuck in a bed-sit with a grumpy landlady, and no other students around you, the weekends could be very long and lonely.

Most institutions give first-year students first claim on halls of residence. But for some students, living with a hundred or so other people, sharing bathrooms, meal times, TV programmes, problems, passions – even bedrooms – can be an unbearable strain. Others thrive on the camaraderie. Criticizing mixed colleges, one student told us: 'Coping with an ex-boyfriend over cornflakes and coffee at 8 a.m. is something not to be endured.'

Getting the right information

College prospectuses will generally give you details about halls of residence, though these may not be altogether bias-free. Student unions may also have a view – ask if there's an alternative prospectus or student union handbook. Above all, check out the accommodation for yourself if you can when you make your first visit.

Look at:

- cost
- whether rooms are shared
- eating arrangements – is it full-board, half-board, kitchen and do-it-yourself?
- facilities provided
- distance from college
- transport availability – and frequency
- shops

Getting help

The college accommodation office is responsible for placing students in halls of residence, and will send you details once you've accepted a place. The accommodation office will also help you to find rented accommodation.

ACCOMMODATION IN HALLS OF RESIDENCE

What will it cost?

If you look at our charts (pages 6–7), you will see that costs vary significantly depending on whether you have full-board, part-board or self-catering accommodation. Costs also vary between universities, with much higher costs especially in the London colleges. Check out exactly what the costs cover and what facilities are provided.

Points to Note:
- Figures for Oxford, Cambridge and Durham are an average for all colleges; costs for individual colleges vary considerably.

- When comparing self-catering accommodation in halls of residence with the rented sector, remember that with college accommodation, gas and electricity are probably included. This is unlikely to be the case in the rented sector.

Will I have to share a room?

Possibly. In some colleges you may have to share a room for one or two terms. If you do have to share, you will probably be sent a questionnaire designed to find out what sort of person you are and the kind of person you could live with. Typical questions: Would you want to share with a smoker or a non-smoker? Are you an early riser? Do you like to go to bed late and get up late? Are you a party person? What kind of music do you like? Is there any kind you can't stand? Honesty is the only way to

---

WHERE DO MOST FIRST-YEAR STUDENTS LIVE?

	All %	Old Universities %	New Universities %	College %
Halls of residence	58	81	29	54
Flat/House	14	5	30	12
Parental home	9	3	10	14
Other	8	6	11	9
Lodgings	7	3	13	6
Bed-sit	2	1	4	2
Hostel	1	0	1	3
No response	1	1	2	0

Source: Higher Education: The Student Experience.

Estimated Weekly Cost of University-Managed Accommodation (FB Full Board PB Part Board SC Self-Catering)

Institution	FB	PB	SC
Aberdeen	£50		£32
Anglia			£35–49
Aston		£47	£31
Bath			£36
Birmingham		£50–65	£22–31
Bournemouth			£40
Bradford		£51–55	£31–55
Brighton		£42–54	£36–43
Bristol		£63	£32
Bristol, University of the West of England			
Brunel			£32–37
Buckingham			£36–48
Cambridge	£54		£50–75
Central England in Birmingham			£25–31
Central Lancashire			£38
City University	£60	£67	£63
Coventry	£60	£52	£40
Cranfield		£46	£35
De Montfort			£30
Derby			£33–43
Dundee		£49	£31
Durham	£63		£34
East Anglia			£35
East London			£25
Edinburgh	£65	£42	£42
Essex			£33
Exeter	£69		£36
Glamorgan		£51	£33
Glasgow	£51	£53	£28–38
Glasgow Caledonian	£63		
Greenwich	£63	£53	£45
Heriot Watt	£54		£30–42
Hertfordshire			£30–45
Huddersfield		£32–58	£35
Hull		£46	£34
Humberside	£60		£32
Keele University	£57		£28
Kent at Canterbury	£54		£35
Kingston			£42–52
Lancaster	£29–32		£31–45
Leeds	£61		£31
Leeds Metropolitan	£49		£30–42
Leicester	£55		£30
Liverpool	£61		£37
Liverpool John Moores			£27–37
London			
Charing Cross & Westminster			£44–54
Courtauld Institute of Art	£75		£33–70
Goldsmiths College		£54–58	£40–45
Heythrop College	£75		£45
Imperial College	£68		£30–53
Jews' College			£50–60
King's College	£76	£55	£51
King's College School of Medicine and Dentistry	£76	£55	£51
London Hospital		£75	£51
Queen Mary & Westfield		£53	£50
Royal Free Hospital		£75	
Royal Holloway	£39–68	£40–59	£46–49
Royal Veterinary College		£75	£30–80
School of Economics		£49–53	£32–59
School of Oriental & African Studies	£56–75		£30–80

continued

	FB	PB	SC
School of Pharmacy	£75		£50
School of Slavonic & E. European Studies		£58	
St Bartholomew's	£68	£60	£50
St George's			£36
St Mary's			£45
United Medical		£72	£37
University College	£61–65		£38–49
Wye College	£65		
London Guidhall		£65	£43–54
Loughborough	£56		£33
Luton	£44		£30–37
Manchester	£56–62		£29–43
Manchester Institute of Science & Technology	£60		£28
Manchester Metropolitan	£58	£58	£38
Middlesex			£45
Napier			£30
Newcastle upon Tyne		£53	£30
North London		£60	£45–55
Northumbria at Newcastle	£57	£44	£36
Nottingham	£58		£28
Nottingham Trent		£63	£45
Oxford	£65		
Oxford Brookes	£73		£42–47
Paisley			£20
Plymouth			£35
Portsmouth	£55	£50	£33
Queen's, Belfast		£51	£34
Reading	£62		£36
Robert Gordon		£42–47	£34–46
Salford		£51	£24–43
Sheffield	£55–80		£32
Sheffield Hallam		£55	£39

	FB	PB	SC
South Bank			£45–50
Southampton	£56–68	£65	£35
St Andrews		£52	£25–42
Staffordshire			£29
Stirling			£30
Strathclyde	£50		£39
Sunderland	£50		£36
Sussex			£38
Surrey			£33
Teeside		£38	£34
Thames Valley			£54
Ulster			£20–30
Wales			
Aberystwyth	£61		£35
Bangor		£48	£34
Cardiff	£36–53	£50	£25–43
Lampeter	£59		£33
Swansea	£59		£30–40
Warwick		£43	£30–45
Westminster			£56
Wolverhampton	£58	£47	£32
York			26

Source *University and College Entrance 1995: The Official Guide*

harmony. Even if you are easy-going about smoking, do you really want to sleep in a smoky atmosphere? And, though your intentions may be very laudable at the moment, how are you going to feel about your roommate stomping around at eight in the morning when you've been out partying until two?

How much is your rented accommodation going to cost?

Research carried out by *Students' Money Matters* in January 1994 in higher education institutions throughout the UK revealed some interesting facts. The average cost of rents in London amongst the students we contacted were predictably higher than anywhere else – on average students were paying £54 pw. Apart from London, in Scotland rents proved to be higher than in the rest of the country at £39 while in England and Wales generally they were £36. Full details of rents in different parts of the country are on pages 14–15.

Cash crisis note:

● Students in the South East, but studying outside London, are thought to be suffering particularly badly, as they are being asked to pay London-equivalent rents while not qualifying for the larger grants and student loans given to students who study in the capital.

● 67 per cent of students said that accommodation off-campus was easy to find. However . . .

● 55 per cent thought it was expensive and around the same number thought it was difficult to find suitable and reasonably priced accommodation close to their university. In London and the South-East many student spent well over half the value of their full grant on accommodation.

● There are of course winners and losers in the accommodation game:
   * while students are no longer eligible for housing benefit to help them through the summer vacation, more and more students are applying to the access funds for help with rent with varying degrees of success. £300 was the highest amount anybody we discovered managed to get.
   * the rapid growth in student numbers has increased competition for rented property traditionally taken by students; however, with many house owners unable to sell their houses because of the recession, there is more property to rent on the market.

Action:
Check out the length and terms of your contract – is it for 52 weeks? A recent survey of university students found that more and more landlords were asking students to sign 52-week contracts for accommodation. This means they are paying rent during the Christmas, Easter and three-month summer vacation, when they are likely to be at home.

What problems do students encounter when renting accommodation?

NAILING THE LANDLORD
Tanya's Story

'*Good rented accommodation in the West End of Glasgow is hard to come by, so when two of my friends and I found somewhere we liked quickly, we were not bothered by the unwillingness of our new landlord to come to any formal agreement. But when he insisted that we paid him in cash, and refused to give receipts, I started to get worried, and went to the Citizens Advice Bureau to find out what our rights were.*

As I had suspected, without any written agreement our landlord would be free to take advantage of us – well, at least kick us out without notice.

An adviser helped me to draw up a tenancy agreement, which expressed the terms of notice, gave details of the amount of deposit we had put down and how much rent we paid; in short everything that the landlord had agreed verbally with us. I also included some extras which I felt would increase our security, e.g. repairs and maintenance of the flat were his responsibility. I then produced four typed copies of this contract which I was able to persuade him to sign. We also started to keep note books in which we asked him to sign when we paid rent. I am doubtful whether he used his own signature, or even his own name; however, when he threatened to throw us out (and worse) we knew that we were protected and these were empty threats.'

'*Landlord hadn't attended to repairs, emptied meters, bothered about moths – holes everywhere.*' Liverpool

'*Most houses are damp. It takes a lot of mould to get a landlord to do anything.*' Sheffield Hallam

'Landlord never got round to returning my deposit. Took him to small claims court. Bailiff said he had vanished – so had my £150.' Postgrad, La Saint Union

'All five of us paid £200 deposit which we never saw again.' Robert Gordon University, Aberdeen

'Damp, not very secure, infestation common, unsafe area, poor furniture – not many complaints.' University of Central England

'Broken into every year for the last three years. Agent took over a week to change the locks.' Sheffield Hallam

'I was stuck in lodgings miles from anywhere. The buses stopped at 7p.m. so studying at the library or staying on campus after 6.30 meant paying for a taxi home.' Brunel

Should I take out insurance?

That's something only you can really decide. You may find your parents' insurance covers you for personal possessions – check that with them first. Otherwise . . .

● If you are living in halls of residence you may well find that there is a comprehensive policy covering all students and your bill will include insurance cover. Check this out before considering taking out any personal insurance cover.

   Endsleigh Insurance is currently offering students in halls of residence cover for £2,000 for £27. Most banks offer special student insurance at competitive rates.

● If you are living in rented accommodation, the landlord of the house or flat you rent should have the premises covered by insurance for fire and structural damage, but it is unlikely to cover your personal possessions. Students tend to keep open house, and because people are coming and going all the time, security is often lax. If you do have a lot of expensive possessions, then it might be worthwhile considering insurance, especially if you carry expensive belongings about. Ask yourself: What would it cost me to replace my stereo, TV, video, camera, gold watch, PC, course books, whatever? Compare that with an outlay of say £35–£60 a year. Rates for personal insurance depend on where you live. It costs more if you live in a big city than a sleepy rural town. And in a crime black spot rates can be prohibitive.

'Insurance is so ridiculously high here – £100 p.a. for £1,000 cover – it's just not worth having and you can't get cover for a bicycle for love nor money. That's what comes of living in grotty area. As far as insurance is concerned we're right off the map. There are better districts of Liverpool to live in but then the rent goes rocketing up so you can't win. The answer is a stout lock on your room door, and have nothing worth pinching.' Student, Liverpool University.

'Everybody round here hires a TV so if it walks it's covered by the TV rental company. The same goes for washing machines and all other appliances.' Student, Liverpool University.

Do I have to pay the Council Tax?

Now the Poll Tax is dead and buried, we have the Council Tax.

Students are largely exempt from paying this. Certainly, if you live in a hall of residence, college, student house or somewhere in which all the residents are students, you will be exempt. If you live in a house where there are already two adults, then your presence does not add to the bill. If you live in a house with one adult, that person will not lose their 25% single occupancy discount providing they can give proof of you being a student.

OTHER LIVING EXPENSES

While your accommodation will probably soak up at least half of your available resources, how are you going to spend the rest?

Food

Once you have a roof over your head, the next major expense is food, and here our survey showed that costs were fairly similar throughout the country with an average of about £16.50 a week. £10 p.w. was a figure often quoted by students as the amount they put into a 'kitty'. The most hungry student we found had a weekly food bill of £45 and was studying in East London.

Socializing/entertainment

Our survey didn't assess how good a 'good time' the students were having, or how often they went out, but for cheapness Welsh students seemed to be managing best, with an average weekly bill of £11.25. Then came Scotland with an average of £18. Elsewhere costs were similar with socializing and entertainment accounting for some £21–£27 a week. Sport was included in entertainment.

Books

All students said they spent more on books in the autumn term and in their first year than at any other time. Some reported that they'd then taken to using libraries instead of buying, as books were so expensive. It is difficult to give an average figure for books, as what you need to buy depends on your course and how well your college library is stocked in your subject. But taking our own survey as a very general guide, the average figure was £59 per term.

Points to check: Your university or college may have a second-hand bookshop. Find out before you start purchasing; books are very expensive. Check out your college library. Is it well stocked in books on your subject? Is it close to where you study and where you live?

Course equipment

In subjects such as architecture, the creative arts and some science based subjects this can be a major item. Figures of £40–£60 a term were often mentioned and £100 for design materials. The highest figure quoted was £150 by a student studying architecture.

Photocopying and stationery

Many students mentioned the high cost of photocopying. For those on courses where study covered topics in a wide range of books rather than majoring on a few text books the cost could be considerable. Figures of £10–£20 per term were mentioned. Stationery was another item which was cited as a significant cost at £5–£15.

Field trips

Geography, biology and zoology students said that field trips could cost anything from around £50 to £345 a time and though they are generally annual rather than termly occurrences, they are a compulsory component of many courses.

Clothing

Average cost: £2.90 per week

As we asked for weekly figures in our survey, the low figure for clothing and the frequency of Nil suggested that it was not a weekly expenditure, more an occasional splash-out. Birthday or Christmas presents and charity shops were often given as an alternative answer. Wry comments such as 'I can't afford it' following a confession that up to £40 a week went on socializing and entertainment suggest that for some students clothes are simply a low priority rather than an unaffordable luxury.

So – where is the cheapest place to study?

'In your first year you go mad. You are very childish. I was spending £20 a week on alcohol and another £10 on cigarettes. But you can't go on like that, physically or financially.' (Roger, Loughborough)

'In my house we cater communally. If you buy food together and cook together, it works out much cheaper – just £12 a week.' (J, also at Loughborough)

In the first edition of *Students' Money Matters*, Wales came out marginally cheaper than other areas. Our research this year puts it top of the league for money management again. Not surprisingly London is the most expensive place to study by far, followed by the home counties. The hardest hit students are those studying just that bit too far outside London to qualify for the higher grant, yet still paying the London prices.

TRAVEL DURING TERM TIME

To survive, it seems you need to be fit. Students said that walking and cycling were major forms of getting about. For many, however, travel was a significant cost, with students in London experiencing the most severe problems in terms of expense and time taken to get to lectures. The average London student spent £12–£15 a week on travel and £22 a week was mentioned by some students. Compare this with Durham students who, because of the smallness of the city, tend to walk everywhere. Students studying Medicine based in London proved to be the hardest hit, as training can often mean attachments to other hospitals with locations as much as 40 miles away. Students in Glasgow also

HOW STUDENTS BUDGET AROUND THE COUNTRY

(Rent – figure given is what students questioned said they were actually paying. Figure in brackets is what they estimated the average price for the area to be)

London		
per week		
Av. rent	£54.46	(£51.42)
Av. food	£24.87	
Av. socializing	£14.72	
Av. entertainment	£10.92	
Av. clothes	£6.25	
Av. toiletries	£3.59	
Av. fuel	£5.66	
Av. telephone	£5	
Total	£125.47	
Av. books (per term)	£70	

Oxford and Cambridge		
per week		
Av. rent	£42.95	(£46.41)
Av. food	£17.50	
Av. socializing	£15	
Av. entertainment	£6.50	
Av. clothes	£2.10	
Av. toiletries	£1.29	
Av. fuel	£5	
Av. telephone	£2.53	
Total	£92.87	
Av. books (per term)	£34.33	

Manchester		
per week		
Av. rent	£36.21	(£36.50)
Av. food	£14	
Av. socializing	£13.21	
Av. entertainment	£7.85	
Av. clothes	£1	
Av. toiletries	£3.41	
Av. fuel	£8.60	
Av. telephone	£3.35	
Total	£87.63	
Av. books (per term)	£63	

Tourist Centres		
(e.g. Bath, York)		
Per week		
Av. rent	£37.41	(£38.77)
Av. food	£16.56	
Av. socializing	£13.70	
Av. entertainment	£13.80	
Av. clothes	£4	
Av. toiletries	£2.29	
Av. fuel	£3.95	
Av. telephone	£2.95	
Total	£94.66	
Av. books (per term)	£43	

Home Counties
per week

Av. rent	£40.16	(£40.19)
Av. food	£17.59	
Av. socializing	£15.64	
Av. entertainment	£6.95	
Av. clothes	£3.27	
Av. toiletries	£3.23	
Av. fuel	£6	
Av. telephone	£5.54	
Total	£98.38	
Av. books (per term)	£57	

Wales
per week

Av. rent	£32.50	(£35)
Av. food	£13.50	
Av. socializing	£8.75	
Av. entertainment	£2.50	
Av. clothes	£0	
Av. toiletries	£2.75	
Av. fuel	£4	
Av. telephone	£2.50	
Total	£66.50	
Av. books (per term)	*Not available*	

West of England
per week

Av. rent	£38.16	(£36.14)
Av. food	£16.37	
Av. socializing	£15.83	
Av. entertainment	£6	
Av. clothes	£1.75	
Av. toiletries	£0.75	
Av. fuel	£4	
Av. telephone	£3.25	
Total	£86.11	
Av. books (per term)	£53	

North
per week

Av. rent	£36.26	(38.40)
Av. food	£14.89	
Av. socializing	£23.00	
Av. entertainment	£6.82	
Av. clothes	£3	
Av. toiletries	£3.25	
Av. fuel	£5.86	
Av. telephone	£3.38	
Total	£96.46	
Av. books (per term)	£50	

Midlands
per week

Av. rent	£33.33	(£31.99)
Av. food	£13.82	
Av. socializing	£21.30	
Av. entertainment	£4.67	
Av. clothes	£3.94	
Av. toiletries	£2.88	
Av. fuel	£7.80	
Av. telephone	£4	
Total	£91.74	
Av. books (per term)	£60	

Scotland
per week

Av. rent	£39.10	(£39.12)
Av. food	£15.21	
Av. socializing	£13.97	
Av. entertainment	£4.35	
Av. clothes	£1.80	
Av. toiletries	£2.66	
Av. fuel	£5.71	
Av. telephone	£3.01	
Total	£85.81	
Av. books (per term)	£62	

seemed to be paying a high cost for travel – on average £8.20 a week. However, Scottish students on a grant can claim extra for travel of over approximately £65 a year. On average other students in the UK pay £5.70 a week for travel.

Travel check

● **The frequency of local bus services**: A huge number of students complained of the infrequency and unreliability of bus services:

> *'There was a bus, but if it turned up, it was always so full of students I couldn't get on. In the end my dad had to buy me a car.' Law Student, University of the West of England*

● **The last bus**: A number of students complained that in many cities bus services finish early, with no regular service after 10.30 p.m. – a major problem for sociable students in outlying districts. Check on this when choosing accommodation.

> *'The last bus was at 7p.m. Hopeless for even the most modest socializing.' Law student, Bristol*

● **The cost of taxis**: If there are a few of you, it might not be prohibitive.

● **What the area is like at night**: A number of students mentioned fear at having to cross parkland from halls of residence with poor lighting and the risk of mugging and 'whatever'. Students in East London complained of badly lit streets where even as early as 5p.m. they really didn't want to walk

Other student complaints

● Exeter students said that short cuts to popular student lodgings were badly lit. Manchester students complained of split campuses with a five mile journey between the two. Some Liverpool students said it just wasn't safe to go anywhere on your own at night.

● Many students complained that cycling was a danger and muggings for mountain bikes was a gripe from Manchester. Students elsewhere complained that theft of bicycles was a problem.

How far do most students have to travel to study each day?

A recent survey showed that while most university and college students managed to live either in or relatively close to their place of study, students at the 'new' universities were not so fortunate.

Miles from place of study	0	1	2	3	4	5	6/more
Old Universities %	58	14	9	6	3	3	7
New Universities %	21	20	16	13	5	5	20
Colleges %	45	13	10	5	3	3	21

Source: Higher Education: The Student Experience.

How much will it cost to get to your college from home?

If you live in Exeter and decide to study in Glasgow, then getting there is going to be a major expense and you won't be popping home very often. But if home is Birmingham and you study somewhere close at hand, like Manchester, then it's relatively cheap. Coaches are always cheaper than trains, but they take longer and the amount of luggage you can take with you is usually limited.

STUDENT RAIL AND COACH CARDS

Both the coach service and British Rail offer student reductions, provided you buy their special student cards. These last for a year. One longish journey will more than cover the initial outlay, which is:

Rail card: £16 (January 1994)
Reduction: one-third off all rail fares.
Travel restrictions: currently – you cannot travel before 9.30 a.m.; there's less of a reduction on Fridays and some Saturdays around Christmas; there are specific restrictions on certain trains. Check with station.

Coach card: £7 (January 1994)
Reduction: one-third off all fares.
Travel restrictions: some journeys cost slightly more at certain times
– e.g. £1 more on a Friday.

Travel advice note

● **Restrictions** on cards can change, so always check what is being offered and when you can travel.

● **Look for special reductions**: occasionally BR or the coach companies will have special promotions such as half-price student cards, or half-price fares.

● **Taxi fares**: you may find that your accommodation is some distance from the railway or coach station. If you have a mountain of luggage, hi-fi, guitar, duvet, books, etc., you will need to take a taxi – another added expense.

Here are some comparative travel costs from London, based on return fare prices in January 1994. Prices quoted include young person's Rail card or Coach card discount:

London to	Train	Coach
Edinburgh	£38.95	£20.50
Newcastle	£36.95	£17.50
Manchester	£21.10	£15
Nottingham	£17.50	£12.25
Birmingham	£15.20	£ 9.25
Cardiff	£19.80	£14
Bristol	£17.15	£12.50

CAN I AFFORD TO RUN A CAR?

If your only income is the standard grant most rational people would say no. But since so many students do seem to have cars they must be managing it somehow. Travel from your home to your university will probably be cheaper by car, but you may also find yourself coming home many more times in a term, acting as chauffeur to the party, and taking trips at weekends. And don't underestimate the maintenance bills: they can be astronomical especially on an old car. Then there's the road tax currently £130 p.a. (which can be purchased half yearly), your MOT, and AA membership which makes sense if you have a tendency to break down. But your biggest outlay will undoubtedly be the insurance.

How much to insure my wheels?

Two wheels or four, it's not going to be cheap or easy.

4 wheels

Students lucky enough to have a car, may find they don't have much luck finding insurance, especially if they are first time drivers and under 21. Endsleigh, says that students are finding it very difficult to get insurance. Until a couple of months ago they would guarantee that they would give the best quote for motor insurance to students. But not any more.

'We will only insure up to a maximum of £3,000 so you are looking at the reliable cheap, slow cars – the Fiesta, Mini, Ford Escort, not the hot hatches such as the XR2, XR3 or Golf GTI. Even then first time insurers with no experience aged around 18 are looking at a premium of £400 upwards', says Ian Stewart of Endsleigh marketing. He also cautions against the old trick of mum taking out the insurance and naming the student as second driver. *'If there's a claim and it's discovered that the student is really the main driver you could find the insurance company won't pay up'*.

Insurance costs vary, depending not just on who you are, but on where you live. Big city drivers pay a higher premium than say country folk. In London the costs are prohibitive. Check out if it is cheaper to take out your insurance from your home address or your university lodgings as Vicky did to her advantage. *'My parents live in London. I am studying in Durham. By taking out my insurance up here I saved well over £50.'*

2 Wheels

Now you might think a bicycle was much easier to insure. But any student thinking of taking a bicycle to a university, must think in terms of having it pinched, or at least borrowed without permission. Insurance companies certainly do.

Insurance Advice
A good padlock and detachable wheel or saddle should be your first form of insurance. Think in terms of exchanging that expensive mountain bike, for something that looks as if it's come off the tip.

Who to try:
Endsleigh. In October 1993, for cover on a bicycle worth £150, they were charging £33 in a good area rising to £57 in the most dodgy. There are parts of Birmingham, Liverpool, Leeds, Teesside and Manchester where you could get no cover at all. But remember you've got to take out personal cover as well.
Banks. Some of the Banks offer a fairly good deal. Midland for example will provide cover for a bike valued at £175 for £31 and Barclays at 17.5 per cent of the value (minimum £24).

VERDICT: expensive but well worth considering if your bicycle is your only means of transport.

TYPICAL STUDENT BUDGETS

Two students from around the country show how their money goes.

Jo, 22, Biology
3rd year, Nottingham University
Accommodation: living out – shared house with three other students, own bedroom.

OUTGOINGS	Per month	Per year	Comment
Rent	£120	£1,260	rent paid for 52 weeks. Half price during 12 weeks of summer.
Electricity	£4.77app	£57.28	
Gas	£9.04	£108.48	Central heating. Always warm. Will increase with VAT.
Telephone	£8–£10	£117	I was alone in the house for the summer and ran up a bill of £45.
Food	£45	£540	We shop and eat together putting £10 each in the kitty.
Additional food	£12	£144	I'm a chocoholic especially at exam times.
Toiletries	£3.50	£42	
Train fares home		£69	Return to Essex 3 times a year £23.
Fares during term	£0	£0	I cycle
Field trip		£100	Portugal to study plant, animal and insect life.
Bicycle upkeep		£20	I also bought a D-lock – £20 it's cheaper than insurance
Socializing & Entertainment	£40	£480	Beer is £1 a pint – student bars. 50p reduction at cinemas.
Clothes	£0	£0	Rely on birthdays and Christmas.
Rail card		£16	
TV licence share		£6	cheaper because black & white
Washing	£6	£72	Use of launderette
Holidays		£130	Germany – special ticket £70. Lived with friends.
Sundries	£7	£84	Once a week I do a soup round among the homeless in Nottingham, if they need something desperately, like the lad last week who wanted a ticket home, well what can you do.
Total		£3245.76	

For Jo's income, see p. 22

INCOME	Per term	Per year	Comment
Grant	£728	£2,265	Next year's students will get less
Additional allowance	£50	£150	Nottingham terms are a week longer
Access Fund		£100	form said you couldn't get it if you hadn't a student loan, but I did.
Earnings		£880	8 week research job in summer (£110 a week)
Total		£3,395	

Additional Comments:

'Nottingham is a good shopping centre and reasonably cheap. I cycle everywhere, so have no travelling expenses. Rents are usually for 52 weeks, but a good landlord will reduce it to half price for the summer months. There are subsidised bars – beer £1 a pint. You can get reductions at cinemas and theatres. Balls cost around £20, not the astronomical sums of Oxford and Cambridge. When my parents saw my house they just said 'oh dear' – well, don't they all. It's not a stately home but I like it. Theft is a problem, especially when the students are away, but I can't afford insurance. A friend of mine beat the burglar by having a room that looked as if it had been done over already, while his tidy house mates lost cameras, stereos, records, the lot. I keep a notebook itemising my expenditure, which is very boring but is probably why I can just make ends meet. I do go out, but fortunately I don't drink – a mammoth saving.'

Benedict, Physics
2nd year, University of Sussex
Accommodation: sharing university managed house with three friends.

OUTGOINGS	Per month	Per year	Comment
Rent	£146	£1,314	University owned, so no rent during 3 summer months
Electricity	£5	£45	over 9 months ⎫ next quarter
Gas	£10	£90	over 9 months ⎭ we'll have VAT
Telephone	£6	£54	over 9 months
Rent of line		£11	
Food	£80	£720	9 months. I go home for the summer.
Travel – Van petrol	£40	£400 approx.	large and thirsty – used for relief trips to Croatia in hols.
Van repairs		£477	Expensive break-down while on aid convoy at Christmas
Motor Insurance		£290	
Socialising	£60	£720	I role my own cigarettes, cutting addiction to £20 a month
Entertainment	£20	£240	
Clothes		£50	Pair of boots – will last for years – saving?
Books		£225	
TV licence	£0	£0	Never watch
Computer Discs		£30	I buy in bulk
Rent owing from last year		£740	halls of residence – 2 terms
Sundries	£5	£60	difficult to gauge
Total		£5,466	

INCOME	Per term	Per year	Comment
Grant		£2,265	
Student loan		£800	also had £700 last year
Earnings:	£200 approx	£1,560	Evenings/weekend Uni bar £40–£60 a week during term.
Help from brothers		£200	Assist with cost of van repairs
Overdraft		£100	Was bigger but wiped out by student loan. Will increase.
Total		£4,925	Expect to work in summer to cover short-fall

Comment:

> *'There's been a property crash in Brighton so it's cheaper to live here than you might think. Try* Yesterday's Bread – *that's what the shop's called and that's what it sells. Also the cheap meat shop – 5lb of bacon for £2. Charity shops and jumble sales are good if you like old records. Beer is expensive, even in student bars – £1.30 a pint. You'll find few alcoholics at Sussex. My current financial problems stem from my last trip to Croatia. We took aid to a refugee camp and hospital. I'm applying to the hardship fund to cover these debts so, fingers crossed, I'll be able to pay off my rent from last year. Even so, I expect to have a debt of around £3,000 when I graduate.'*

How much of a problem is finance to students?

If you talk to students, you soon realise that money is not just *a* problem but *the* major problem. Even students who were not yet in debt, and so seemed to be managing fairly well, felt that it was their major worry. Though money is top of the list, it isn't the only problem first-year students in higher education encounter, as the findings from this survey reveal.

Students were asked to list the three problems they felt were most worrying:

PROBLEMS	%
Financial	71
Examination anxiety	41
Lack of confidence	37
Depression	34
Relationships	30
Career/course indecision	27
Anxiety	26
Homesickness	24
Housing	22
Loneliness	17
Alcohol	10
Parents	6
Sex	4
Drugs	2

Source: Higher Education: The Student Experience.

WHAT THE STUDENTS HAD TO SAY

'I was very fortunate to get into halls – a real blessing. There is always someone's door to knock on.'

'The social life is centred around drinking. If you don't drink, making friends can be more difficult.'

'When I got my grant cheque, I went totally mad. Going to the disco – not on books!'

'My grant came really late – it was a crisis!'

'Finances are the big problem. Students go out and spend madly in the first few weeks. Then they realise that it's gone. They go to the bank and ask for more. Most don't know where it's gone.'

'Be honest when filling in the accommodation form. You might end up sharing with someone with whom you have nothing in common.'

CASH CRISIS- COST SAVINGS

- Don't shop on an empty stomach – it's fatal.
- Always telephone during the cheap rates – after 6 p.m. or at weekends in the UK and after 8 p.m. for overseas calls.
- Watch out for special coach company offers.
- Check that water rates are included in your rent.
- Look for special student nights at night clubs, theatres, cinemas.
- Check out student union shops; they buy in bulk and so give good discounts. Beer, stationery, dry cleaning, even holidays could be part of their cost cutting service.
- Buy books second-hand.

So how much are you going to need to survive as a student?

£3,000? £4,000? £5,000? Leeds University Union are advising their foreign students coming from abroad that they'll need at least £6,500 and the NUS estimates that UK students will need £5,075 in London and £3,733 elsewhere for the 38 week academic year for 1994/95. You'd be lucky if you had that. In reality you're going to have to survive on what you can get and what you can earn. How much is that likely to be? Read on!

2
WHERE WILL THE MONEY COME FROM?

Main sources of finance for undergraduates

In this chapter we look at the main sources of finance for students embarking on higher education –

- fees
- grants
- loans
- access and hardship funds
- the banks
- funds for for disabled students

– and how to set about getting them

FAST FACTS ON FINANCE

Fees:	paid for most degree and HND students.
Grant:	£2,560 in London, £2,040 elsewhere, £1,615 living at home (slightly less in Scotland), means-tested on parents' income.
Student Loans:	£1,375 in London, £1,150 elsewhere, £915 living at home – less around 27% in your final year.
Access Fund:	random distribution depending on college; given largely to help with rent and other financial hardships.
Study abroad:	some additional help from LEA and other schemes.

FEES

Who will pay my fees?

Your Local Education Authority if you live in England or Wales. Otherwise the Scottish Office or the Department of Education in Northern Ireland will pay your fees, provided both you personally and your course are eligible. Fees are not means-tested, so payment is not affected by parental income.

How will my fees be paid?

They will be sent direct to your college.

Will all students living in the UK get their fees paid?

No. You must have been a UK resident for the three years before your course begins. Being temporarily away from the UK – say, because your parents were working abroad – does not count as breaking your residency.

Will the local authorities automatically pay my fees for any course I take at any college?

No. Courses where fees *will* be paid include: full-time (including sandwich) degree, HNC, HND, Postgraduate Certificate of Education, or equivalent courses undertaken at a UK university, publicly funded college or comparable institution.

Courses where fees will *not* automatically be paid include: school-level courses such as A levels or Scottish Highers, BTEC and ScotVEC National Awards and City and Guilds courses, postgraduate courses (except teacher training), nursing courses in the 'Project 2000' scheme, all part-time courses (except initial teacher training courses), correspondence and Open University courses.

What can I do to raise funds if my fees are not paid?

1 Apply for a discretionary grant – see next question.
2 Apply for a Career Development Loan – see question after that.
3 Apply to professional bodies, trusts, foundations, benevolent funds – see Chapter 5.

I want to take a course where fees aren't automatically paid – what can I do?

Local Education Authorities have the power to offer 'discretionary grants'. These can cover just fees, part of fees, full maintenance or part maintenance. There are no hard-and-fast rules as to how such grants are distributed, or to whom. Each local authority decides on its own policy, and each student's case is very different. In some areas discretionary grants are competitive, so your examination results could play a significant part in your success; or you might be limited to taking a course within your local area.

What are Career Development Loans?

They are designed for people on courses of up to two years where fees aren't paid and cover course fees (only 80% given if you are in full employment) plus other costs such as materials, books, childcare and living expenses. You can apply for up to £8,000. The scheme is funded by a number of high street banks and administered by the Employment Department who will pay the interest on your loan during training and for up to one month afterwards. If the course you take lasts more than two years you should contact your local Training and Enterprise Council who may be willing to sponsor your career development loan for more.

For a free booklet on Career Development Loans phone 0800 585 505

What's my position as an overseas student?

Unless you are from the EC, or can get your own government to pay your fees, you are expected to pay them in full. Legally you can be charged higher tuition fees than UK students – so you can be thinking of a minimum of £5,500 p.a. for an arts course, £7,360 p.a. for a science based course and £13,550 for a clinical course. Most universities and colleges do have a designated overseas adviser who you could contact. The rules are different for EC citizens (who pay the same fees as UK students), refugees, new immigrants and EC migrant works. If you are already in the UK, contact the educational enquiry service at the British Council Information Centre, 10 Spring Gardens, London SW1A 2BN Tel: 071 389 4383. Otherwise try the British Council, High Commission or Embassy in your own country.

MAINTENANCE GRANTS

What is a maintenance grant?

A maintenance grant is the money paid to students by their local authority to live on while they are studying.

Does every student get one?

No. They are means-tested, generally on your parents' income.

Are grants really being cut?

Yes. In the budget at the end of 1993 it was announced that student grants were to be cut by 10 per cent in each of the next three years starting in the academic year 1994–5. This means the figures given for 1994–5 will be cut by a further 10 per cent next year, and another 10 per cent the year after. To compensate for this reduction, the loan that students can take out will be increased (see details page 49). So, by 1996–7 the grant and loan will be roughly equal, in other words students will be expected to pay roughly half their own maintenance costs. In all situations there are winners and losers.

The winners – parents who were having a struggle paying their contribution towards the grant, will now find their student children can borrow more.

The losers – students who will have to pay more towards their own maintenance costs.

This book does not set out to argue the rights and wrongs of the students' situation, its function is to provide information. Not surprisingly, however, our research revealed strong feelings about the 10% cut among students. Here are a few of their more printable comments:

> *'I was sitting after a lecture having a quiet cup of coffee when a student friend arrived in a revolutionary frenzy. "You've got to come on the grants march" – she seemed really upset – "it is the first time the whole of Scotland has marched in protest. It's really important."' (Glasgow University)*

> *'Students will be leaving with larger and larger debts because of the decrease in grants. We can't let the government get away with it!' (University of East London)*

'Lack of parental contribution already makes life impossible. I live on half what I should. Books need subsidising.' (Brunel University)

'University – it's more a big survival struggle than an academic challenge.' (Brunel University)

'A 10% grant cut will make things extremely difficult, perhaps even force people to leave.' (Bath University)

'Stronger and stronger feeling that students from poorer families are being penalised by the system. By definition poor students are being forced into more debt.' (Glasgow University)

'Many current undergraduate friends have said they would not have contemplated university if conditions had been like this when they started their studies.' (Glasgow University)

'At the moment I just survive on the full grant and nothing extra, this won't be possible any more.' (Nottingham University)

What is the full maintenance grant?

The rates for a full grant for students living in England, Wales or Northern Ireland for 1994–95 are:

- £2,040 p.a. if you are living away from home and studying at a college outside London;
- £2,560 p.a. if you are living away from home and attending an establishment within the London area;
- £1,615 p.a. if you are living at home.

Rates for students from Scotland are:

- £1,975 p.a. if you are living away from home and studying outside the London area;
- £2,495 p.a. if you are living away from home and attending an establishment within the London area;
- £1,480 p.a. for students living at home.

Why are Scottish grants lower?

Because the full cost of travelling expenses is not included. Scottish students can claim for travelling expenses over a certain amount. The figure last year was around £60–£65, but has yet to be set for this year.

Will I get a grant?

Getting money out of anyone is never easy, and the government is no exception. To give you some idea, we looked at the latest figures available for full-time, dependent students in England and Wales, 1992–93:

Nil maintenance	23%
Some maintenance	35%
Full maintenance	24%
Remaining 18% were independent students	

How much a student is entitled to depends on how much their parents (or spouse) earn – and remember: they consider your parents' joint income.

How do they calculate how much grant I am entitled to?

The actual calculation of how much your parents are expected to contribute towards your maintenance – if any – is very complex, and based on their 'residual income': that means what's left after essential expenses have been deducted.

So what are essential expenses? It works like this. The LEA takes your parents' gross income and then subtracts allowances for things like interest payments (mortgage up to £30,000), dependants (including gran or other adult, if their income isn't over £1,875), pension schemes, life assurance, and superannuation payments that qualify for tax relief. A disabled parent can also claim for domestic help.

To take a very simple example, if your parents earned a gross income of £28,000 and their only deduction was their mortgage payments which amounted to £3,000 a year, their residual income would be seen as £25,000. They would then be expected to contribute £1,093 towards your upkeep, so you would get a grant of £225 in London and just £57 in the rest of the country. It is likely that most families would have more deductions than just their mortgage.

The local authority generally looks at your parents' last year's income. But if this has suddenly taken a tumble your parents can always ask to be assessed on their current earnings.

What happens if my parents are not prepared to divulge their income?

Then you will get no grant from the local authority. This, however, will not affect your fees.

To claim a full grant, how little must my parents earn?

To claim a full grant, your parents must have a combined residual income of less than £14,845 (1994–95 figures).

To get any grant, what is the maximum my parents can earn?

If you are the only child in the family in higher education living away from home, then the cut-off point for your parents' residual income is between £32,000, and £38,000 depending on where you are intending to study and live. But remember: it is residual income, so actual earnings might be substantially more.

What if I have a brother or sister who also wants a grant?

If there are several children in the family in higher education, all claiming maintenance grants, then the parents' residual income can be much higher, as the parental contribution is divided proportionately between the children. For example, if there were two students in one family, both attending a college outside London, their combined grant could be £4,080. As you can see from the chart (p. 34), the parents' residual income would need to be over £45,000, and their gross income substantially more, before they got no help at all.

Does the parental contribution ever change?

Yes. The threshold at which parents begin to contribute towards maintenance was raised in 1994 from a residual parental income of £14,345 to £14,845, and the rest of the scale was adjusted accordingly. At the same time, however, the student grant was cut by 10 per cent. So, where does that leave parents?

GRANT CALCULATION CHART

Contribution scale for students entering higher education after 1994

Parents' residual income £	Parents' contribution £
0–14,844	nil
14,845	45
15,000	57
20,000	508
25,000	1,093
30,000	1,737
35,000	2,462
40,000	3,186
45,000	3,911
50,000	4,636
58,032 or more	5,800

Contributions are calculated as follows:
Residual income

From £14,485 to £18,974	£1 in £12.00
From £18,975 to £27,884	£1 in £8.55
From £27,885	£1 in £6.90

In reality their 'expected' contribution was cut by 10 per cent too. So, for example, parents with a son studying away from home in London, who decided to play it strictly by the rules and contribute up to the maximum amount of the current grant, would be £285 better off and the student £285 the poorer. It is unlikely that the Government's intention in cutting the grant was to let parents off the hook, and one hopes parents who can afford it won't take advantage of the new situation, but those are the facts.

What if my mum or dad is made redundant?

If your parents' income suddenly drops, then your grant will need to be recalculated, and you should contact your Local Education Authority, or Awards Branch immediately.

If my parents can't afford to or won't pay their share of my grant, is there anything I can do?

No. There is no way that parents can be made to pay their contribution towards your grant, and the local authorities will not make up the difference. The National Union of Students estimate that around 45–50 per cent of students find that their parents do not pay their full contribution. In Austria parents are taken to court if they don't pay their share of the means-tested grant, but not in the UK. And, contrary to student mythology, it is no good getting your parents to write to your local authority saying they have kicked their student child out and are no longer giving them house room, in the hope of getting a full grant. A spokeswoman at the DFE assured us: *'We are up to that one. The Government has left no loopholes unclosed. Nice try!.'*

It can come as rather a shock to parents when they discover just how much they are expected to fork out, especially if the student's course covers four years. If you get no LEA assistance, then you could be thinking in terms of well over £6,000–£10,000.

'Education had always been free for us, and we thought when our daughter went to university things wouldn't be any different. So it came as something of a body blow when a few weeks before she left for the North we discovered she would get no grant at all and we were going to have to dig deep and find the full maintenance contribution of £686 a term. By then it was too late to start thinking of universities closer to home.' (Helen Wolf, London)

Are there any circumstances when my parents would not be asked to contribute towards my maintenance grant?

Yes – if you:

● are 25 or over
● have been married for at least two years
● have been supporting yourself for three years
● are an orphan
● are in care.

I want to go to a University in my home town, but don't want to live with my parents – can I get a full grant?

Students living at home are eligible for a reduced grant only (£1,615 p.a.). If your home is within ten miles of your chosen university or college then your Local Education Authority will see no need for you to live in lodgings, even if you do, and usually only give the lower 'home rate' grant. However, if you can make a good case for the need to live away from home, such as transport problems or personal health reasons, then you can appeal.

I'm thinking of getting married – will it affect my grant?

Not immediately. But if you have been married for over two years, your partner, provided he or she was earning enough, would be asked to pay up. The 'spouse's' contribution starts at a lower rate of residual income than for parents, and is significantly higher – see chart. The reason given by the Department for Education for this obvious spouse discrimination is that your partner is likely to gain more from your higher education than your parents. It has a kind of logic. Still, we understand that the system is under review.

Spouse's residual income £	Spouse's contribution £
11,745	10
15,000	369
20,000	965
25,000	1,734
30,000	2,588
35,000	3,559
40,000	4,530
46,539 or more	5,800

I'm an overseas student, can I get a grant?

No. Even students from the EC classified as 'home' students as far as fees are concerned are generally not eligible for a grant or a loan.

When should I apply for my fees and grant?

England/Wales: As soon as possible, though not before January for a course starting the following autumn. Application forms should be available from your school, otherwise from your Local Education Authority. You do not need to wait to be accepted by a university or college to apply.

Scotland: When you receive an unconditional offer from a university or college. Application forms are available from your school and Awards Branch from April for courses starting in the autumn.

Northern Ireland: No need to wait for a firm acceptance – apply as soon as possible. All completed forms should be at your local Board Office by the end of May for courses starting in the autumn – by the end of June at the very latest.

What is the grant meant to cover?

Lodgings, food, books, pocket money, travel.

Note: in Scotland the grant is slightly less, as it covers only travel up to £60 (figure under review). Excess travel costs may be claimed using Form AB4, available from your university or college.

My academic year is longer than at most colleges – can I claim any extra grant?

Yes. If your course is longer than 30 weeks 3 days in any year (25 weeks 3 days at Oxford and Cambridge), you can claim extra from your local authority. The full rates in 1994–95 are:

London	£74.05 p.w.
Elsewhere	£55.45 p.w.
Living at home	£38.90 p.w.

If your course year is 45 weeks or longer, then you will receive a grant based on 52 weeks.

Are there any other allowances I could apply for?

Yes.

1. Travelling Expenses *England and Wales:* the first £231 of any travelling expenses if you live at home, and £149 if you live away, must be met from your grant. Above that you can claim.

Scotland: if living away from home 3 return journeys per year to your place of study can be claimed for plus additional term-time travel to and from your institution. (This does not include students whose parents live outside the UK) First £60 of claim will be disregarded. Living at home – Maximum paid £2.60 per day plus £540 (figures under review).

2. Older Students If you are 26 or over and have received in benefit or income £12,000 in the last three years you can claim:

	England & Wales
26 years	£300
27 years	£535
28 years	£800
29 years or over	£1,045

3. Two homes allowance Maintaining a home other than the home you live in to attend the course – £635

4. Dependants

Spouse	£1,820 max
other adults	£1,820 max
children depending on age and circumstances	£385 to £1,820

If I work part-time, will it affect my grant?

No. Students can work during their course – i.e. undertake vacation work – and the money earned will not be considered when their grant is calculated. However, sandwich course students who undertake a year's *paid* industrial training will not receive a grant during that year. It is estimated that over half of all students work during the vacation.

Is there any kind of income that could affect my grant?

Yes. If you received more than:

- £3,865 from a scholarship or sponsorship, or from your employer
- £1,810 from a trust income
- £3,030 from a pension, except a disability pension
- £800 from other sources (this does not include vacation work).

How will my grant be paid?

Maintenance grants are paid in three termly instalments. A cheque is sent to your university or college for collection at the beginning of each term. You will be told beforehand how much to expect.

Panic! My maintenance cheque hasn't arrived!

It happens – not that often, but it can be dramatic when it does. In an ideal world your cheque should be waiting for you when you arrive at your university or college, but things can go wrong.

Typical reasons we discovered:

● the local authority computers went down, so the cheques didn't get out on time;

● local authorities were behind with their workload;

● students applied late for a grant, so the amount of the grant had not been assessed;

● the university lost the cheque.

Whatever the reason, it doesn't help the destitute students to eat, so . . .

What can I do if my grant doesn't come?

● **Try the bank**: If you already have a bank account, then the bank may help you out with a loan – talk to the Student Adviser at the campus or local branch. This, of course, is no help to the first-year student who needs a grant cheque to open a bank account.

● **Try your LEA**: If the hold-up is caused because your grant allocation is still being calculated, you can ask your local authority for a provisional payment.

● **Try your college**: Ask your college for temporary help. Most institutions have what's called a hardship fund set up to cover just this kind of eventuality.

● **Try Access**: Finally, there are the Access Funds which have been set up to help students. Full details of these are given later in this chapter.

● **Friends?** They may well take pity on you when it comes to socializing, buying you the odd drink, but it is rarely a good idea to borrow from friends.

CASH CRISIS NOTE 1
As you will not be able to bank your maintenance grant until you have arrived at your university or college, you will need to have some money of your own to get yourself there, and possibly to maintain yourself until the cheque is cleared. Check out the cost of train fares.

CASH CRISIS NOTE 2
If you are living in halls of residence, then your college will probably be sympathetic if your cheque hasn't arrived and will wait until it does. But don't be too sure about this – check it out. Some colleges will add a penalty of as much as £20 to the bills of students who don't pay up on time.

CASH CRISIS NOTE 3
If you are living in rented accommodation, you can expect no leniency. Landlords expect to be paid on the dot, and usually ask for rent in advance. You will need funds to cover this.

I have to spend part of my course studying abroad – will my grant be increased?

Living costs in different countries vary, so grants are adjusted to cover this. There are four categories:

● **Highest-cost countries**: these include Denmark, Finland, Japan, Norway, Sweden, Switzerland and Taiwan.

● **Higher-cost countries**: these include Australia, Austria, Belgium, France, Germany, Iceland, Hong Kong, Korea.

● **High-cost countries**: Canada, Indonesia, Italy, Luxembourg, New Zealand, the USA, Russia plus other countries previously in the USSR, Republic of Ireland, the Netherlands, Spain.

● **All other countries**.

While students studying in the 'all other countries' category will receive the normal grant, which remains unchanged each year, those visiting the high-cost to highest-cost countries will find that their grant is increased each year. The full rates for 1994–5 for England and Wales are:

Highest-cost countries:	£3,485
Higher-cost countries:	£2,990
High-cost countries:	£2,510
All other countries:	£2,040

My course abroad is longer than my course in the UK – can I get more money?

Yes. The rates given here are worked out on a year of only 30 weeks 3 days (25 weeks 3 days for Oxbridge). If you need to stay longer, then you can claim more. Rates for 1994–5 per week are:

Highest-cost countries:	£103.60 per week
Higher-cost countries:	£87.80 per week
High-cost countries:	£71.90 per week
All other countries:	£56.00 per week

It's going to cost me a lot more to fly to Tokyo than to take a train to Leeds – can I get any help with travel?

Yes, but you won't get full reimbursement. Your grant already includes some travel element (£149 for full grant in England and Wales), and this will be taken into consideration in calculating how much you receive. It is probably best to let your local authority calculate what you are entitled to. Remember, when putting in for costs, to give all the facts – that journey from your home to the airport costs something too.

Note to higher-earning parents: While your earnings might disqualify your son or daughter from claiming any maintenance grant while they are based in this country, if they are studying in one of the high-cost countries you may qualify for some help. This is not spelt out in the Department for Education leaflet, so check the figures with your local authority. It's always worth a try.

Is there any other help for students who want to study abroad?

Three organizations have been set up to assist students wanting to study in the EC:

COMETT (Community Programme for Education and Training in Technology) is concerned with forging closer links between industry and higher education institutions, in particular through advanced training in technology. Grants are available to help undergraduates and newly qualified graduates, studying technology-based subjects, who want to undertake periods of training and work experience in industry in other EC or EFTA countries.

ERASMUS is designed to encourage greater co-operation between universities and other higher education institutions within the EC, and provides grants for students to help with the cost of study in other EC countries.

LINGUA, which promotes the teaching and learning of foreign languages, is aimed primarily at students who are following foreign language courses or where a foreign language is a major component of the course. Assistance is given to students seeking to study abroad.

Who to contact

Funding from these organizations is arranged mainly through your university or college. They should have full information and should, therefore, be your first point of call. Otherwise contact:

The European Commission – London Office: 8 Storey's Gate, London SW1P 3AT. Tel: 071–973 1992. Ask for their booklets *Finance from Europe: A guide to grants and loans from the European Community*, and *Guide to the European Community Programmes in the Fields of: Education, Training, Youth*. Otherwise contact the individual organizations direct (see addresses below).

What happens if I get sick while studying abroad?

Don't wait until you get sick, take out health insurance cover before you go. (See details under travel insurance on page 118) Your local authority will probably reimburse the costs of health insurance providing they consider it 'economical'. Check out the situation with them first or ask for advice from your university before you take out any insurance cover. Remember, above everything else, to hold on to your receipts. Without those you are unlikely to get any reimbursement from your local authority.

Thoughts of a marcher demonstrating against the cuts in grants in Scotland:

'In debt to the bank and the student loans company already, and worse to come, the pressure to get a job, any job, as quickly as possible when you qualify is enormous. And with so few jobs of any kind around, many graduates are asking themselves why they bothered. Coming to university is a daunting prospect for anyone, but the thought of debts that will take years and years to repay is enough to deter many students. Increasingly we will see a return to an elitist system of education with only those students who have parents rich enough to support them attending university. Arts and humanities will be abandoned as non-marketable. If graduates are taking the jobs that non-graduates would formerly have taken then the nation's workforce will gradually become over-qualified for the positions they hold and everyone will become dissatisfied. Keep marching!'

Where can I find out more about grants?

Full information about grants is given in the following free booklets, which you would be well advised to get and study.

For students in England and Wales:
Student Grants and Loans: a brief guide
Department For Education, Publications Centre, P.O. Box 2193, London E15 2EU. Tel: 081-533 2000

For students in Scotland:
Student Grants in Scotland, available from any Scottish University. In case of difficulty, contact the Scottish Office Education Department, Gyleview House, 3 Redheughs Rigg, South Gyle, Edinburgh EH12 9HH. General Enquiries: 031-244 5823. Failing that 031-244 5870

For students in Northern Ireland:
Department of Education for Northern Ireland, Rathgael House, Balloo Road, Bangor, Co. Down BT19 7PR. Tel: Bangor (0247) 270077

For Welsh speaking students:
>Welsh Office Training, Enterprise and Education Department, 3rd Floor, Companies House, Crown Way, Cardiff, CF4 3UT. Tel: 0222 388588

COMETT Liaison Office, Department for Education, Sanctuary Buildings, Great Smith Street, Westminster, London, SW1P 3B7, Tel.: 071-925 5000

UK ERASMUS Students' Grants Council, University of Kent, Canterbury, Kent CT2 7PD. Tel.: 0227 762712

LINGUA – as for ERASMUS

LOANS

Are students really expected to exist on just over £2000 a year?

Of course not. The grant is now only half the story, or at least it will be by 1996. In autumn 1990 the student loan was born, and with it a new attitude in this country to the financing of students through higher education.

The student loan: What are the 'real' facts?

When first introduced the newspapers were full of stories about the rights and wrongs of the student loans scheme. Some thought that education in this country should be completely free; others that students should contribute to their education. There are forceful arguments on both sides. More recently the discussion has centred on whether or not graduates should contribute towards their fees through a tax on income after graduation. So far there has been no decision.

Whatever your views, and whether you like the idea or not, if you are in higher education in this country you will probably end up having a loan. So here are the practicalities.

As we said earlier in this chapter, grants for students have been reduced. To bridge the increasing gap between the amount you get through your grant or your parents and the amount you need, a special loans company has been set up to provide additional finance for students. There is a fixed amount students can borrow each year from this loans company, set at the amount they are thought to need.

So while the grant decreases the amount you can borrow through the loan scheme will increase each year. Eventually the student loan will constitute half your maintenance needs – in other words, students will be expected to pay half their own maintenance costs. What the government of the day decides to do in 1996 when we get to a 50:50 situation is anyone's guess. But for now, unless you have rich and generous parents, a job or a private income, all students will be expected to have a loan of some kind.

Compared with your predecessors' situation, it's tough. But undoubtedly those who will be starting their courses a few years from now will think you had it relatively easy.

In the first year of the Student Loans Scheme, around £70 million was paid out to fund over 180,000 students. In the second year £139 million was paid out to 261,000 students, and by 1992–93 £226.5 million was loaned to over 345,000 students. Already the student loan scheme is an integral part of student finance.

Is it right or wrong?

When the student loan scheme was first introduced obviously it caused a lot of controversy as shown by these quotes from students at the University of Westminster on a BBC Radio 4 programme:

'I really didn't want to take out a loan and hung out to the end, but I needed to clear my overdraft. So I had to eat my words and take one out anyway.'

'If you take out a loan in your first year, second year and third year, by the time you leave you have an enormous debt to pay off and it is a bit of a deterrent to students to come to university. If you drop out of your course halfway through and you end up with an enormous debt and no degree, you're going to be in a bit of a state.'

'It's quite a frightening thought when you're only 20 years old to say: "Oh, I'm borrowing all this money – what chance have I got of ever paying it back?"'

'I should be concentrating on finishing off my course and looking towards my career. As it stands, I have to worry about the pressures of money and having a court summons brought up against me for debts and suchlike. It is very difficult to concentrate sometimes.' (a 21-year old third-year student who had failed to pay his credit card bill and had debts mounting to £3000).

While some students interviewed thought it was only fair that they should partly fund themselves rather than place the burden on the shoulders of the state, others thought the government was going the wrong way about attracting more people into higher education.

Today's students are much more reconciled to the situation of being in debt as a recent survey carried out for Barclays Bank by the NUS shows:

Attitude to debt by final year students:
Worried –   5%
Concerned –   11%
Angry –   34%
Resigned –   36% (an increase of 16% on the previous year)
Pleased –   14%

However, students who took part in the *Students' Money Matters* research had this to say:

> *'No matter how careful you are with money you will still be in debt and having £3,000 debt hanging over you isn't the best way to start a career.' (Brunel University)*

> *'We need more money not less! It's an outrage.' (Robert Gordon University, Aberdeen)*

> *'It's exceedingly difficult trying to maintain a reasonable standard of life – student finance is crap.' (York)*

> *'Don't let the lack of finances deter you from going to university.' (La Sainte Union)*

> *'If I can't find a job in the vacations, I have a problem affording to eat.' (University of Central England)*

This book does not set out to argue the rights and wrongs of how students are financed through higher education – we leave that to others. Our aim is to give you hard information on how to juggle your finances and tap every source available so that you can cope in the current economic climate.

HOW DO BRITAIN'S STUDENTS FARE COMPARED WITH STUDENTS IN OTHER COUNTRIES?

Judge for yourself.

When it comes to funding students through higher education, it would seem that no country has found the perfect solution: some countries provide loans, others grants, and the rest a combination of both – and the permutations are endless.

If you are looking for a common approach from our continental neighbours, forget it. Almost all students in the Netherlands get assistance, while in France hardly any do. When it comes to levels of loans available, there are big differences too: a student in Norway can pick up over three times more than a student in Denmark, which may seem hard until you realise the Danish student is cushioned by a generous grant.

To make things worse, nobody seems to be satisfied, so just when you are beginning to get systems sorted out, countries will change things. Germany abolished grants in favour of loans in 1984, but is now thinking of bringing them back in some kind of dual system.

Sweden has been tinkering with its system continually for twenty-five years, moving from a grants system to an almost entirely loans system, and now swinging back in favour of grants again. Recently it has increased the grant portion of the total amount paid out to students to 30 per cent. Even so, most students graduate with a massive debt. Around £9,000 is common. For those studying medicine or engineering it will be considerably more.

In Australia, there is a mix between means-tested grants and loans, similar to here, but all students are required to pay back 23 per cent of their tuition costs. So looking for the differences in systems is easier than seeking comparisons, as you'll see from the five systems reviewed here:

France: Fees are low, around £150 a year, but students have to pay them. They also, generally, support themselves, as grants are not widely available. 'Hardship' students can get help with living expenses, based on parental income and the number is increasing, but this funding can be withdrawn if performance is not satisfactory. Loans are given only in extreme circumstances. There is high public funding on subsidized food (70 million meals) and accommodation (100,000 beds).

Germany: Fees are paid by the state and students can attend the university of their choice, even changing institution at will during courses. In West Germany during most of the 80s the state provided interest-free long-term loans for needy students (around 33 per cent). However, since 1990 financial assistance has been on a fifty-fifty basis: half grant and half loan which is means tested. The loan repayment begins five years after graduation and extends over twenty years. From this year East Germany has been brought in line with West. The majority of students need part-time work to help finance themselves.

Denmark: Students in Denmark are considered independent at the age of 18 and so all are eligible for a grant if they go to college. This ranges from £90 a month for those living at home to £300 a month for those in lodgings, with the additional option of a loan of around £120 available. Interest rates on government loans are 4 per cent during the course and 8 per cent once qualified. While the cost of living in Denmark is slightly higher than in the UK students can just about manage on the grant, providing they don't party every night.

Belgium: All grants are means-tested on parents' income, but those who receive a full grant should find it enough to live on. There is no system of loans so Belgium students do not generally get into debt. Belgium is a small country so many students live at home and those that live away generally go home at weekends. Accommodation costs are not as expensive as in the UK. All students have to pay an enrolment fee of around £50 a year for their course and if they don't get a grant parents have to pay this. Courses are generally longer than in the UK: 2–3 years for non degree courses, 4–5 for degrees.

Sweden: A mix of grants and loans provided by the state. Assistance is means tested but only on the student's own income. Parents' or spouse's income is not taken into account. The non-repayable grant is about 30 per cent of the total amount (currently about £155 a month), with the rest (£405 approx. a month) given as a loan. Interest is fixed annually by the government and is currently 8.7 per cent. 'Payback' is set at 4 per cent of income with repayments beginning within six months of finishing the course. At least 88 per cent of students have a loan. In the main, Swedish students are better off than their counterparts in the UK, but their debts are massive.

America: Students are responsible for paying both their fees and living expenses. Typical cost of a course with full board is £10,000 p.a. The US Government does not support higher education at all. Because of this, students often have jobs during term time and work their way through college. The long summer break is designed so that students can earn enough money to pay for the academic year ahead. Financial aid is granted to more talented and under-resourced candidates. Special loans are available to all students.

HOW STUDENT LOANS WORK: THE FACTS

Who can get a loan?

The loans are intended largely for students undertaking full-time first degree or Diploma of Higher Education courses at universities or colleges of higher education. There are a few anomalies, such as the Certificate of Qualification in Social Work and certain paramedical courses, so it is always worth checking. Loans are not means-tested, so provided you are attending the right course, no matter what your income or your parents' income is, you can get a loan.

Can overseas students get a loan?

The short answer is no. You will need to have met certain residency criteria.

How much can I borrow?

The loan is reviewed annually and, like the grant, is dependent on where you are studying. In the year 1994–95 the rates are:

	full year	*final year*
Students living away from home & studying in London	£1,375	£1,005
Other locations	£1,150	£840
Students living at home	£915	£670

Every year a new rate is fixed, depending on inflation. The increase for 1994–5 on the previous year was approximately 40 per cent.

TOTAL STUDENT RESOURCES FROM GRANTS AND LOANS FOR 1994-5				
Students living away from home and studying in:		*Basic Grant*	*Loan*	*Total*
London	full year	£2,560	£1,375	£3,935
	final year	£2,560	£1,005	£3,565
Other locations	full year	£2,040	£1,150	£3,190
	final year	£2,040	£840	£2,880
Students living at home	full year	£1,615	£915	£2,530
	final year	£1,615	£670	£2,285

Why are the rates lower for the final year?

Because they do not cover the summer vacation. You are expected to be working by then, or can draw Social Security. However, if your final year lasts 40 weeks or more you can get a loan at the full rate.

I'm studying abroad – can I get a loan?

Yes. If you study or work abroad for a full year as part of your course you are eligible for the 'elsewhere' locations rate. If you are normally based at a London college and away for less than a year then you can apply for the higher rate.

When can I apply for a loan?

Once you are attending a higher education course you can apply for a loan. You can reapply each year once the autumn term has started. Applications can be made at any time during the academic year. However, there are two important dates to remember:

30 June: colleges are not obliged to certify your eligibility for a loan after this date, and you do need that certification to get a loan.

31 July: loans will not be issued after this date.

When is the best time to take out a student loan?

There are three options:

1 When you need it.
2 As late as possible because it's index-linked to inflation (see page 52 for explanation).

3 As soon as possible. We hear some financially astute students are taking out their student loan, even if they don't need it, and investing it in a good interest-paying account with a bank or building society. These generally pay more than the inflation rate. Make sure you know what you are doing. Check out interest rates first. Ensure you can get at your money quickly and easily if you are likely to need it – some of the high interest rate accounts give limited access.

How do I get a loan?

The forms needed to apply for a loan are available from your university or college. An adviser will probably also help you to fill them in. If you were born in the UK you will need your birth or adoption certificate. If you were born abroad you should bring your passport, or a letter or document which gives details of your place and date of birth. Your bank or building society account number is also needed.

Do I have to take out the whole amount?

No. You can take out however much you want up to the maximum for that year, but you can make only one application a year. So if you do not take the full amount, you CANNOT apply for the rest later.

Who runs the scheme?

A government-owned Student Loans Company has been set up to administer the loans scheme. It is based in Glasgow.

When do I have to pay back the money?

You can start paying the money back as soon as you like, but you won't be asked to start repaying your loan until the April after you complete or leave your course, and then only if your income is 85 per cent of national average earnings, which at the moment is about £14,000. Each year the Government sets a level of monthly income under which you can put off repayments. For 1993–94 it was set at £1,165.

Is the loan interest-free?

Yes, but you will have to pay back more than you borrowed in actual money on the table, though not in real terms. Confused? This is how it works.

The amount you borrow is index-linked to inflation. So if, for example, you borrowed £940 in the first year of a three-year course and the annual inflation rate was 1.2 per cent, you would be asked to pay back the loan at a rate of £16.82 per month for a period of 60 months starting in the April after you graduated. The total repayment would be £1,009.20.

The likelihood is that you would need to borrow a little more in your second year, and possibly about the same in your third.

If I'm doing a four- or five-year degree, and so borrow more, will I have longer to repay the debt?

Yes. While most students are expected to repay their loan within five years, those who borrow for five years will be given seven years to pay it off. You can, of course, repay your loan sooner if you wish.

OK – sixteen quid a month won't break me, but in reality it's going to cost a lot more?

Yes, it is likely to be at least three times that amount, and more than likely a lot more. It is impossible to give you any exact figures, as nobody knows what the inflation rate is going to be – or, in fact, how much the loan is likely to increase. But to give you some idea: if we take the example in the previous paragraph and multiply it by three to cover the three years, the amount borrowed would be £3,027.60; your repayments would then be £50.46 a month. If that sounds scary then go back four questions – with earnings of £1,165 a month, you should be able to afford it. But remember these are not accurate figures, and the grant has been increased by almost 40 per cent this year, but it gives you an idea.

It sounds as if all students will graduate to a massive debt – is that so?

Yes, most students starting a course now will have to face up to the prospect of starting work with a debt to pay off, and this could be substantially more than the amount totted up under the Student Loans Scheme. Our research shows that 62 per cent of students had overdrafts, some 56.8 per cent had student loans, and a massive 83 per cent expected to be in debt to either the bank or the Loans Company, or possibly both, by the end of their course – to the tune of £500 to over £5,000

Estimated student debt

17%	No debt
13.5%	less than £500
13%	£500–£1000
17%	£1000–£2000
22%	£2000–£3000
12%	£3000–£4000
3%	£4000–£5000
2%	over £5000

Do the pay-back rules ever change?

They are reviewed every year. With the loans this year up around 40 per cent and likely to increase substantially for the next two years to cover the cut in grants, we have been assured that the Government will be looking very carefully at the rules to make sure graduates can, realistically, pay back what they owe.

CASH CRISIS NOTE 1
Check out Chapter 6 on budgeting – it might save you a few sleepless nights.

CASH CRISIS NOTE 2
Compare current bank overdraft rates for newly qualified graduates.

Will I be able to pay it all back?

As well as the possibility of graduating to a massive debt, most students graduate to a fairly substantial salary. Starting salaries for a 21-year-old graduate with a good second-class Honours degree in 1993 averaged £13,004. If you are earning around £1,000 a month, the repayments won't seem quite so grisly. But will you find a job? And are you going to be a 2:1 success story? At the time of writing this book, the employment market for graduates in the UK is beginning to recover. In fact 7 per cent more new graduates are likely to be offered jobs in 1994 than in

1993. This was the finding of a survey carried out among employers by the Association of Graduate Employers. But, before you start the celebrations, there are likely to be 14 per cent more of you graduating. By the time you qualify, things might be better. It's worth remembering that if you can't find work, the Student Loans Company will wait for repayment; the banks, however, may not be so sympathetic.

I'm a graduate with a £3,000 student loan to clear – is my new employer likely to pay it off?

When the loan scheme first came in, many employers thought they might need to offer the 'carrot' of paying off students' loans if they wanted to attract the best graduates. Whether the government was hoping that employers would step in and clear students' debts in this way was a question often discussed in the national press. In fact at least one major company did draw up contingency plans for such a scheme, and a number of companies we contacted said they were watching the market and their competitors very closely. Then the recession hit the UK hard, graduate openings were in short supply, and graduates were competing for jobs rather than employers competing for graduates. Employers put all ideas of 'loan pay-off schemes for students' on the back burner, so the 'golden hello' hasn't materialized yet. But watch the trends: market influences change very rapidly. In fact one major company we contacted over sponsorship was actively considering whether the 'golden hello' was a more cost effective way of attracting the best graduates than sponsorship. It's certainly something to bear in mind when you're looking for employment, possibly in a few years' time.

Is the Student Loans Scheme better than borrowing from the bank?

Most banks and building societies will give students overdraft facilities on special terms, which often include an interest free £400 overdraft facility which is likely to be increased – so check with the bank. This is intended mainly to help you during that difficult period when your grant hasn't yet arrived. The overdraft is wiped out as soon as the grant cheque is cashed. It is better to use the 'interest free four-hundred' facility if your financial problems are temporary or you are certain you will be able to pay it back once you graduate. Banks also offer students longer-term loans at competitive rates which should be investigated.

But, in general, banks are not the best bet for long-term borrowing for students; the Student Loans Scheme is. (See details on pay-back arrangements in previous questions.)

It's worth remembering, however, that to get a loan you have to have a bank account. If you already have an overdraft with your bank, as soon as the loan hits your account it will automatically be used to pay off the overdraft, so you might not actually find that you have more cash in hand to spend, though you'll certainly have more peace of mind.

"600 Face Court Over Student Loan Debt"

Did you see the headlines in the newspapers? Could that be you? The stories were high on drama but low on facts. Firstly, no student is ever forced to pay back a loan – you have to be in permanent employment and earning at least £14,000 a year and even then, at the most, your repayments are likely to be around £50 a month which should be affordable (1993–4 figures). A spokesman from the Department For Education suggested that the problem was '*not so much can't pay as won't pay*'.

But it's unlikely to be as simple as that in all cases. Perhaps in addition to a student loan, students have run up massive bank overdrafts which also have to be paid back. Perhaps, too, they took out a graduate loan to get themselves kitted up for work. Borrowing money isn't difficult, but borrow too much and paying it back is. The Loan Company said that their greatest problem was communication: '*People just don't tell us what they are earning or that they have fallen out of work, so we assume they can afford to pay.*'

Is there any way I can get out of repaying the loan?

Yes:
- if you haven't paid it off after twenty-five years, or when you reach the age of 50, whichever is earlier (60 if you started your course at the age of 40 or over). Repayment defaulters are always liable.
- if you die!

Where can I get more information?

Call the Student Loans Scheme Help Line on 0345 300 900.

All calls on this number are charged at local call rates, no matter where you are calling from.

The Student Loans Company is based at 100 Bothwell Street, Glasgow G2 7JD.

Full information about the Student Loans Scheme is set out in a leaflet issued free and updated each year from:

Postgraduate Awards: DFE Publications Centre, Department for Education (FHE3), Mowden Hall, Staindrop Road, Darlington, County Durham DL3 9BG.

Scottish Education Department, Gyleview House, 3 Redheughs Rigg, South Gyle, Edinburgh EH12 9HH. Tel.: 031–244 5823; Fax: 031–244 5887.

For Welsh Speaking Students: Welsh Office Training, Enterprise and Education Department, 3rd Floor, Companies House, Crown Way, Cardiff, CF4 3UT. Tel: 0222 222885.

Department of Education for Northern Ireland, Rathgael House, Balloo Road, Bangor, Co. Down BT19 7PR. Tel.: Bangor (0247) 270077. Fax: 0247 456451.

For Blind Students: braille and cassette editions, RNIB, PO Box 173, Peterborough PE2 6WS. Tel: 0345 023 153.

There are many anomalies within the scheme which we have not touched on here. The Student Loans Company issues its own leaflet, and do take advice from your college so that you know exactly what you are getting involved in.

HELP FROM YOUR UNIVERSITY OR COLLEGE

There are a number of special funds you could tap if you get into real difficulties, for example **Access Funds** and **Hardship Funds**.

What are the Access Funds?

Access Funds are sums of money allocated by the government to educational institutions to help students who get into financial difficulties. There are three funds: one covers further education students, another undergraduates and a third postgraduates. The allocation to any institution is based largely on its number of students and local housing costs.

Why were they started?

The Access Funds were first introduced to help students out when they were no longer entitled to claim Housing Benefit and Income Support, and to ease the introduction of student loans.

Currently, the amount allocated to the funds is £28.5 million. Divided between the whole student population, this isn't a vast amount. At the time of writing, it is unknown how much the funds will be next year, and for how long the scheme will continue.

What can I get Access money for?

There are no rules and regulations laid down as to how Access money should be distributed. Handouts are decided purely on the whim of individual institutions and what in fact they feel their students' financial problems are.

Access Funds have been used to help students with:

- rent
- childcare responsibilities
- setting up crèches
- adult dependants
- single parents
- travel expenses
- expenses if they are too old to qualify for a loan (over 50)
- bursaries
- the cost of fees

Some institutions allocated 80 per cent towards rent relief; others as little as 40 per cent. Some insist that you must already have applied for a student loan; others stipulate a rent over a certain figure. At Coventry University, where rents aren't a major problem, 75 per cent of the money is allocated in fixed sums to students with childcare responsibilities, while the other 25 per cent goes into a hardship fund to cover the 'unexpected' – like a burglary. So its something of a lottery whether you qualify for Access, and individual college criteria can change from year to year.

To whom should I apply for money from the Access Fund?

The university or college you attend or have applied to. Ask at the Student Support or Student Services office, or the student union.

GLASGOW STUDENTS IN CRISIS

Neil, 4th Year, Philosophy

'I moved into a flat with friends, fortunately found through the university accommodation office. The rent was £35 per week each and we were all on grants. By the end of the first term I had fallen behind with my rent. By the time the summer came round I owed £700. The university allow debts to accumulate but won't let you matriculate at the start of the next year unless you have paid off the debt. This is so students can work over the summer to pay off their debt. As I couldn't find sufficient work to support myself over the vacation and cover my debt, I was unable to matriculate in the October. That meant I couldn't use the library or other university facilities. Eventually the accommodation officer helped me to work out a monthly repayment plan, but the strain really showed in my work.'

Claire, 3rd Year, English

'I was having money problems but didn't want to ask my parents for help. A friend suggested that I approached my university adviser for advice. He suggested applying to the common bursaries fund. To do this you have to send in details of your weekly expenditure debts, income etc. My adviser also wrote a letter. Luckily my case was accepted and I got £200 – enough to sort out most of my problems'

Francis, 3rd Year, History and Politics

'I had been living in the flat for eighteen months when I reached crisis point. I had no money, my overdraft was at its limit and the landlord wanted the two months rent I owed him. Then, surprisingly, he came up with the solution – he offered to pay ME £5 a day and let me off my debt on condition that I painted the communal hallway. Sounds like a great deal, I thought. But after six hours a day painting I'm not so sure.'

Pippa, 2nd Year, Art

'Imagine the scene: we had been living in the flat for seven months. It was home and we were comfortable. Then out of the blue a messenger arrives on the door step with a 24 hour eviction notice. Background: apparently the landlord had been pocketing our rent – which we had always paid in full and on time – instead of paying the mortgage. Final act: the mortgage company repossessed the house and we had to leave the next day. We had no protection because they had become the new landlords and our lease was redundant – it was most unsettling.'

Gordon, 2nd Year, Latin American Studies
'When I came to university I had an electric guitar, an amp, a bass guitar, a stereo and a camera. In times of financial need these have all had temporary lodging in the pawn shop. Gradually this became less and less temporary so that now I no longer have a bass guitar, a camera or a stereo. The loss of the latter is no great hardship as I have already sold my records one by one to the second-hand record shop.'

How do I set about getting Access money?

Every institution will have a different procedure and different criteria for measuring your needs. You will most probably have to fill in a form giving details of your financial situation. Most institutions will have somebody to help and advise you. They may even have a printed leaflet giving you details.

When should I apply?

As soon as possible. The Fund is limited to the amount that is allocated, so it is largely first come first served. We have heard of institutions that have allocated most of their funds by the end of November of the academic year.

I'm a student from abroad – can I apply for Access money?

Sorry, but no. The Access Funds are restricted to 'home' students only, so overseas students will not be eligible.

What are Hardship Funds?

Hardship Funds are administered by many institutions, and also by some student unions, to help students in real financial difficulty. They all vary depending on the institution, and will pay out money for a variety of reasons.

What help will they give?

Priority is often given to students who are suffering financially because of unforeseen circumstances such as a death in the family or illness.

Sometimes small amounts are given to tide you over or to pay a pressing bill, or to assist with childminding expenses. Increasingly, hardship payments are taking the form of an interest-free loan, which can be especially useful if your grant cheque doesn't arrive on time.

Leeds University Union, for example, offers a range of financial assistance to students who find themselves in difficulty. There is a Fundraising Group which considers all applications. As the money mostly comes from external charitable trusts their hands are tied to some extent because they are governed by each individual trust's guide-lines and criteria. But they are successful as the extracts from the following letters prove.

'My English is not good enough to express my heartfelt thanks to you. When I first met you, I was in despair . . . I owe it to you that I can continue my study here.' First degree student from abroad.

'I am grateful to you and your fundraising committee for your help. With this financial assistance, I can continue my PhD study and research work at this University.' Postgrad in Electronic and Electrical Engineering Department.

BANKS, OVERDRAFTS, LOANS, FREEBIES

Which bank? What's the carrot? What will they do for me?

Despite all the talk of students and their financial difficulties, and our research showing that most students are likely to be in debt by the time they qualify, banks are still falling over themselves in an effort to gain your custom. Nearly all offer students some kind of carrot to get them to open an account, and promise some kind of interest-free loan. Their reasoning isn't difficult to fathom. Banks are in the business of long-term investments. Students are the country's potential high earners. Statistics show that people are more likely to change their marriage partner, than their bank. The strategy is: Get 'em young and you've got 'em for life.

So what's on offer?

Most banks keep their new student offer under wraps right until the very last minute – largely so that their competitors can't top it with a better inducement. This means the new offer is on the table from around June/July. Some banks have a closing date for their offers which could be as early as November, when the first grant cheques have been happily banked. The offer is generally open only to first-year students. Before giving you the benefit of their freebies, the bank of your choice will ask for some proof of your student status such as your Local Education Authority award letter or your first term's grant cheque.

To give you some idea of what you can expect, and to check the next round of offers, we looked at how students fared last year.

Not so well as in previous years it would seem. In terms of cash or cash in kind, ahead of the field were NatWest and the Midland offering £25 (reduced to £15 after October). Next came the Royal Bank of Scotland with £10 cash and Barclays with a £10 Our Price Voucher or clock or sports bag. Lloyds proffered a £16 student rail card and TSB four free cinema tickets and a free driving lesson.

But should one be bribed into choosing a bank? Forward-thinking students may well decide that interest-free overdraft facilities carry more weight in making the choice than a paltry one-time cash offer. Here you would do well to look carefully at the small print before making a decision, for whilst most banks offer the facility, in some banks the free interest offer to students is only available for the first year. Check our chart.

Looking even further ahead, what will your bank's attitude be to your overdraft once you qualify? How long will they give you to pay it off? What will the charges be then? How long does the interest-free loan last?

Recent research carried out by Midland Bank showed that the proximity of the branch or cash dispenser was just as important to most students as the freebies offered.

'I went for the freebies – £30 of record tokens – rather than the most sympathetic bank manager – bad move when debt loomed.' Tanya, Glasgow.

Picking a bank: the student's choice

Most students in England and Wales choose one of the 'big four' banks, they all have branches on or near college campuses and students are well served. Nat West have the most customers followed by Barclays and in third place, but closing the gap fast, is Midland. Lloyds trail in fourth. Midland, Nat West and TSB have reciprocal arrangements that allow customers to use any of their cash machines.

SO WHAT'S THE BEST BANKING BUY?

Compare the current facilities offered by some of the major banks.
The figures were current as at March 1994
N.B. Student packages are usually revised each summer, so check with the banks for the latest information

	Bank of Scotland	Barclays	Clydesdale	Lloyds	Midland	NatWest	Royal Bank of Scotland	TSB
Free banking:	Yes, to within agreed overdraft.	Yes, (some charges: check small print).	Yes, if within credit or agreed overdraft.	Yes.	Yes.	Yes.	Yes, provided you stay within limit of arranged overdraft.	Yes.
Interest on current account:	Yes, when in credit.	Yes.	Yes, paid quarterly or half-yearly depending on account.	Yes, paid monthly.	Yes: paid monthly.	Yes.	Yes, at same rate as current account holder, paid quarterly.	Yes, variable on credit balances, paid yearly.
Free overdraft:	Up to £400. Preferential rates after that.	£400 for first year of study.	Up to £400.	Up to £400 right up to graduation, plus special low rate if you need more.	Up to £400 on request, £700 for 3rd year.	Up to £400 on request, £500 for 3rd year.	Up to £400 in first year if prearranged.	Up to £400.
Student Adviser:	No.	In nearest campus branch.	Yes, nearest campus branches.	Nobody specific.	Yes, in all campus branches.	Yes; called Student Services Officer.	In some branches.	Nobody in particular.
Low-cost graduate loan:	Yes; overdraft up to £1500 at special rates.	Yes, up to £2000, available up to 6 months after graduating.	Yes, up to £2000 for up to 6 months after graduating.	Yes, up to £3000 with 36 months to pay it back.	Yes, up to 20% of starting salary – no maximum, or can be used to convert overdraft into loan.	Yes; no limit stated. Repayment deferred for 4 months.	Yes; £300–£2000 at reduced rate of interest with 4 years to pay back. Repayments can be deferred for 9 months.	None.

	Bank of Scotland	Barclays	Clydesdale	Lloyds	Midland	NatWest	Royal Bank of Scotland	TSB
Special loans for Medicine, Dentistry, Optometry, Veterinary Science:		Professional Study Loan up to £3000.	Up to £6000.		Yes, on application.	Up to £3000.		
Cash point outlets:	Bank of Scotland plus Royal Bank of Scotland, Lloyds, Barclays.	Barclays plus Lloyds, Royal Bank of Scotland, Bank of Scotland.	Clydesdale plus NatWest, Midland, TSB.	Lloyds plus Barclays, Royal Bank of Scotland and the Bank of Scotland.	Midland plus NatWest, TSB, Clydesdale, Northern.	NatWest plus Midland, TSB, Clydesdale, Ulster, Northern and Irish Banks.	Royal Bank of Scotland plus Lloyds, Barclays, Bank of Scotland.	TSB plus NatWest, Midland, Clydesdale.
Insurance:	Preferential rates – cover up to £4000 and £1500 cover for damage to landlord's property.	Special deal negotiated for students.	No special package.	Special student package.	Special student package.	Student protector policy	No special package.	No special package.
Freebies:	Commission – free travellers cheques and foreign currency.	£10 'Our Price' music voucher. If application for Barclaycard approved, choice of clock radio, lightweight rucksack or lecture portfolio.	£30	Young Person's Rail Card, for this or next year. Commission – free travellers cheques and foreign money.	£25 cash up to 1 October, £15 after.	£25 cash. Eurocheque card, commission – free travellers cheques	£10. Free Eurocheque card.	4 free cinema tickets free driving lesson, discount in many shops.

Independent research confirmed Midland as increasing its share of customers faster than any other bank in 1993. Over the border you'll find the two leading Scottish banks neck and neck – the Royal Bank of Scotland and the Bank of Scotland with around 30 per cent of the market each.

Check out:

- ease of getting an overdraft;
- rates of interest charged if overdraft goes beyond limit, and ease of extending it;
- interest rates on graduate loans – some are much better than others;
- what happens to your overdraft once you graduate;
- Proximity to university/lodgings of local branch;
- reciprocal cash point facilities close to your institution – otherwise you could be charged for making withdrawals;

NB Don't choose your bank just because it offers the best freebies.

What is a Student Adviser?

A Student Adviser is somebody within the campus branch of the bank, or the branch closest to your college, who has been earmarked to deal with student problems. They are usually fairly young, and they are always well versed in the financial problems students face. Certainly you will find them sympathetic, and full of good advice on how to solve your particular problems. But you won't find them a soft touch, as one Student Adviser pointed out: *'It's no good us handing out money like confetti, it just builds up greater problems for the student later on.'*

CASH CRISIS ADVICE NOTE:
Never run up an overdraft without asking the bank first. They are much more sympathetic if you put them fully in the picture. And unless they know you are a student, you could find you miss out on the interest-free loan. Talk to your bank's Student Adviser – ideally, before you hit a problem.

What is a graduate personal loan?

This can be a life-saver for the newly qualified graduate. It is a special personal loan scheme offered by some banks to graduates to help tide them over the first few months while they get settled into a job. Midland, for example, offer up to 20% of the starting salary (no maximum) over two years. The loan could be used to pay for suitable clothes for work, a second-hand car, advance rent – whatever you need. But remember: nothing is for free, and if you already have a student loan and a substantial overdraft, this might be just too much debt. The graduate loan should not be confused with the many other types of loans banks offer to postgraduates to assist with study. (See Chapter 6 page 152–4)

HEALTH COSTS

I'm sick and myopic, and I've got toothache – can I get free treatment?

As a student you don't actually qualify for any help, but as someone on a low income you could qualify for **free or reduced**:

- dental charges
- glasses
- eye tests
- prescriptions.

Form AG1 . . .

. . . is the starting point, available from the DSS or post office. That will probably send you off on a trail leading to Form AG2, AG3, and AG5, and don't forget to ask for receipt form FP57 (EC57 in Scotland) to claim for free prescription charges. If you are confused, and who isn't, then Leaflet AB11 will put you straight on the NHS and P11 on prescription charges.

Try to get things going before treatment begins, or at least before you need to pay up. Otherwise, make sure you keep all bills and receipts, as evidence of costs. If after filling in AG1 you are told you are not entitled to any help and you think you are, give the DSS a ring, it could be that the computer is 'confused' as well – it has been known. It can be a long process, but it's often worth the effort.

HIGHER EDUCATION AND THE DISABLED

I'm disabled, and I want to go into higher education – can I get extra help?

Yes. There are a number of ways that you can get extra help, depending on your disability. If you follow up every lead offered here, it's going to take time, but the results could be well worth while.

What's the starting point for somebody disabled?

First choose your course, then choose the university or college where you would like to study. Next check out the college facilities, and their ability to cope with your specific disability, by:

1 writing for details of facilities;
2 visiting suitable institutions;
3 having a 'special needs' interview with the institution.

Finally, fill in your UCAS application.

When should I start getting organized?

Early in the summer term of your first A-level year, as you may have to revise your choice of institution several times.

What financial help can I expect from my Local Education Authority?

Like most students on full-time higher education courses in this country, as a disabled student you would be eligible for a mandatory grant. This would pay for your tuition, examinations and registration fees. You may also be eligible for a maintenance grant; this, however, is means-tested and depends on your income or your parents' income (see details earlier in this chapter).

For courses that do not fall within the ambit of the mandatory grant, discretionary grants are given, but this will depend very much on the generosity of your Local Education Authority.

I am severely disabled – can I get a student loan?

Yes. As an undergraduate you would be eligible for a student loan regardless of probable earning capacity and therefore repayment ability once qualified. In fact, the regulations laid down when the Student Loans Company was set up allow for the loans administrator to delay the start of repayment and/or allow a longer repayment period for people with disabilities. If you earn less than 85 per cent of national average income, repayments will be deferred. Phone the Loans Company Help Line on 0345 300 900 (all calls charged at local rates) for more details.

Can I apply to the Access Fund?

Yes. Each institution decides on its own criteria for Access payments, so exact entitlements would depend on where you decide to study. You might even find being disabled gives you an entitlement. See Access Fund details in this chapter.

What extra money is available for disabled students?

There are three Disabled Students' Allowances:

1 Up to £4,730 per year for non-medical personal help – e.g. readers, lip-speakers, note-takers.
2 Up to £3,560 per course for specialist equipment – e.g. computer, word processor, Braille printer, radio microphone, induction loop system.
3 Up to £1,185 per year for general expenses – e.g. minor items such as tapes, Braille paper, higher heating, clothing or dietary expenses, extra use of telephone by the visually impaired, extra books or photocopying.

All allowances are means-tested. Most authorities will require receipts or a quotation before you can claim the allowance.

Can I get extra for travel?

The mandatory grant includes a set amount for transport costs – as a disabled student you can claim for extra travel expenses incurred if your disability means, for example, that you are unable to use public transport and must travel by taxi.

What about Social Security benefits?

It you qualify for the Disability Premium, the Severe Disability Premium, are receiving the Disabled Student's Allowance because of deafness, or are already receiving Income Support, then as a disabled student you could be eligible for Income Support or Housing Benefit. The ifs and buts are never simply explained. The people to put you in the picture are your Social Security office or SKILL, the National Bureau for Students with Disabilities (see below).

Can I get a Disability Allowance?

This new allowance replaces the old Mobility and Attendance Allowances, and it is available to you as a student. It provides funds on a weekly basis for those who need help with mobility – e.g. the cost of operating a wheelchair or the hire or purchase of a car. It also covers those who need care and assistance with any physical difficulties such as washing or eating, or continual supervision. The allowance will not affect your grant in any way.

How else can I raise more money?

There is a wide range of trusts and charities which provide funds for the disabled. These are covered in Chapter 5: Other Sources to Tap.

Who to contact for advice

- Students' Welfare Officer at your university or college, Students Union, Local Citizens Advice Bureau.

- SKILL, The National Bureau for Students with Disabilities, 336 Brixton Road, London SW9 7AA. Tel: 071–274 0565. They run a special information and advice service, and publish a number of useful leaflets and books for the disabled.

- Welfare Rights Office or local Social Security Office; address should be in your local telephone directory.

- Disablement Income Group, Unit 5, Archway Business Centre, 19–23 Wedmore Street, London N19 4RZ. Tel: 071–263 3981

- Royal National Institute for the Blind, 224 Great Portland Street, London W1N 6AA. Tel: 071–388 1266.

- Royal National Institute for the Deaf, 105 Gower Street, London WC1E. Tel: 071–387 8033.

3
SPOTLIGHT ON SPONSORSHIP

A complete guide to getting sponsorship, and what to expect from it

Probably the best and most comprehensive way of raising extra finance to help you through higher education is sponsorship.

- What is sponsorship?
- How do you get it?
- What do you get?
- When do you get it?
- What do you have to give in return?

In this chapter we turn the spotlight on sponsorship, on the changes to the sponsorship market that have been taking place recently, and on some of the companies most likely to give it.

What is sponsorship?

You've heard of big companies sponsoring events such as the London Marathon, the FA Cup and cricket. It means that they back the event with money. In the same way, companies sponsor students through college.

What would sponsorship mean to me?

In financial terms, it would probably mean that you would be £37 a week better off than your contemporaries at college, with guaranteed work during the summer which would bring in a further £1,400 or more. But it's not all for free, and sponsorship is not just about money – it also includes work experience and training.

FAST FACTS ON SPONSORSHIP

Who gives it:	Major companies
When:	For a full course After 1st year of study After industrial placement For final study year
To whom:	Degree and HND students – all subjects, but largely Engineering
Most sponsored subject:	Engineering – Mechanical, Electrical/Electronic
Most generous sponsors:	Paper and Packaging,
Largest sponsor:	GEC
What it's worth:	£600–£2,000 p.a. approximately
Other plus points:	Work experience – industrial placement
Will it secure a job?:	Helpful, but no guarantee

How do I get it?

1 You apply to a company which offers sponsorships. These are generally offered to students doing specific subjects.
2 You are offered sponsorship as the result of a period of work experience.

What subjects should I take if I want sponsorship?

ENGINEERING: Has to be top of the list by far in the quantity of opportunities. The latest figures we have show that one in every four Engineering students is sponsored. Rewards vary. If it's financial rewards you're after, then undoubtedly London Underground and paper and packaging are among the front-runners, but it can't be stressed too much that experience for engineers is very often a vital component of their degree course, and this must be uppermost in your mind when you are looking for a sponsor. The greatest number of sponsorships are for students on Electrical and Electronic Engineering and Mechanical Engineering courses.

COMPUTER SCIENCE: Another well-represented area but

demand is down. Of the 61 engineering firms we checked offering sponsorship, only 12 listed computer science.

BUSINESS STUDIES: The up-and-coming subject when it comes to recruitment, but sponsorship opportunities are right down. To be fair, most firms sponsor only a few Business Studies students, and some not every year, but it's always worth a try. Many companies have tacked sponsorship for Business Studies students on to their existing sponsorship schemes for engineers. If you are trying to maximize on financial rewards, it could be worth looking at companies where the sponsorship scheme was started to attract people to an unpopular, unglamorous or very specialized industry. Companies particularly interested in Business Studies students are McDonald's and Marks and Spencer. See also GEC plc and British Steel.

MATHS AND PHYSICS: There is a demand, but it's not that great. If you sift through company lists, you will find there is a need.

LANGUAGES: Even with Europe on every managing director's mind, there is no real demand for pure language students. You might, however, be fortunate with companies that are making it big in Europe.

OTHER DISCIPLINES: You may be lucky – a few companies, such as Barclays Bank and Arthur Andersen, will sponsor people on any degree course, but you have to be interested in finance.

Who gives sponsorship?

Employers – largely to those studying for Engineering degrees, but a limited number of sponsorships are available for Arts and Science students. Increasingly sponsorships are being given to students in Business Studies, Finance, Retail and Information Technology. The three Armed Forces also sponsor students.

Sponsorship of students in universities and colleges has been going on for many years. It was originally started to attract more young people into engineering. Even today engineering is still the major area where sponsorship can be found. Latest figures (1992) show that 90 per cent of student sponsorship is for Engineering students, and some 70 per cent of Engineering undergraduates receive some kind of award, through increasingly for only the final year.

When could I get sponsorship?

● After A levels or BTEC for a full degree or HND course.

- After a Gap year spent with a company, between A levels and higher education.
- After your first year of study.
- After a successful period of work experience or an industrial placement year.
- For your final year of study

While a large number of sponsorships are still given to A-level students for their full three to four years of academic study, more and more companies are choosing to sponsor students later in their degree course, when a commitment to the subject has been established. There are two major reasons for this: (1) companies were finding that their retention rates among sponsored students were not good; (2) the recession has meant fewer job opportunities for graduates, so less competition for the best talent.

Jim Herrington, Schools Liaison Officer of the IMECHE and editor of Sponsorship and Training Opportunities in Engineering, says:

'The sponsorship market has changed considerably just in the last year. Many of the smaller organizations who only want one or two sponsorship students are now going straight to the universities of their choice and asking for who they want. This is largely to avoid having to deal with the thousands of applications which advertising in our publication would engender. In a way we have shot ourselves in the foot by being so successful. While there are fewer sponsorship opportunities, there are some good sponsorships around which are still well worth going after.'

How does sponsorship work?

There are no hard-and-fast rules – every company devises its own scheme. In principle it works like this:

As a sponsored student you would get training, work experience and financial help while at college to varying extents, depending on the company scheme. You might be asked to work for a whole year in the company either before or during your course; you might be expected to work only during the summer vacations.

In return, the sponsor gets the opportunity to develop close ties with 'a potentially good employee' and to influence your development. There is generally no commitment on either side to employment after the sponsorship. However, since the company has invested a considerable amount of money in you as a student, it is unlikely not to offer you a job.

What would I get financially?

There are many types of sponsorship. Generally, the sponsorship will include a money grant given to the student while he or she is studying, and some form of paid work experience which is generally at the going rate for somebody of your age.

Why do companies give sponsorships?

We canvassed some 150 employers. The reasons most often given were:

● access to high-quality students before they graduate with the hope of future employment;

● opportunity to assess students over a longer period as potential employees;

● chance to develop a student's skills and have an input into their training;

● the grapevine effect: publicizing our company among other students.

Here are some companies' comments on sponsorship:

'Enables us to recruit high-calibre people and encourages more people to work in engineering.' (GEC Marconi)

'Creates greater understanding of chartered accountancy among undergraduates.' (Arthur Andersen)

'Provides a steady stream of young graduates who will hopefully go on to become the leaders of tomorrow.' (NatWest)

'Attracts good-quality candidates for employment after graduation.' (British Coal)

'Never underestimate the grapevine effect. If you treat a student well during sponsorship, others in that university or polytechnic come to hear about it. Of course, the same happens if you treat them badly.' (Digital)

'Opportunity to see trainees in work situations before graduation – it's like a four-year assessment.' (BPB Paper and Packaging Ltd)

'Input of fresh ideas into the company. Able to assess students as future employees.' (Avon Rubber PLC)

'Gives students a chance to look at us and we to look at them, so if offered a

job they will know the company – warts and all – and will stay a long time.'
(British Nuclear Fuels)

Who gets sponsorship?

Employers are – quite naturally – looking for the brightest and best students to sponsor; they want to have the pick of the potential high-fliers at an early stage. When many students first apply for sponsorship they have only their GCSE results and a headteacher's report to show what they are capable of. This can be tough on those who wake up academically after GCSE or who really excel only in their one chosen subject. But good employers are more aware than you might expect; selection is not on academic qualifications alone. Sponsors are looking for signs of those additional qualities needed to succeed in your chosen career: leadership potential, the ability to grasp ideas quickly and to work within a team. They want ambitious, innovative, get-up-and-go people who can think for themselves and get things done. So if your GCSE grades slipped a bit – or, as one student we interviewed put it, 'you look like Mr Average on paper' – think through what else you have been doing. Playing in the football or hockey team; helping out at the local club; hiking across Europe; getting a pop group together – it could help to redress the balance. Remember: the application form is the first weeding-out process, and you are up against stiff competition. This is no time for false modesty – you've got to sell yourself for all you're worth.

The application form

Views on the application form from the sponsored and a sponsor:
'There were all the usual questions on the application form plus some tricky ones like "What has been the highlight of your life so far?"

If you're an obvious candidate – straight As for all A levels, or you have a glowing report from your headteacher – then you're probably OK. But if, like me, you're Mr Average, you've got to make yourself stand out.

I tried to inject some humour into it. A tricky question for me was "What work experience have you had?" With school on Saturdays, the answer really was none. Still, I had helped out a friend who runs a high-class hot-dog stand, if you can have such a thing. I described him as a entrepreneurial capitalist, and where they asked: "What have you learnt from this experience?" I put "Saying 80p in fifty different languages". This was remembered; so was I.'
(Richard Barnes – a sponsored student with Ford, studying Mechanical Engineering at Southampton University.)

'At Barclays the first round is obviously the application form. It is very detailed, very structured, and has to be completed by October. They ask about your interests, part-time work, responsibilities held. It certainly helped focus my mind for my UCAS form later on. There were three reasons why I think they decided to interview me. Firstly, I had been on an exchange to the Soviet Union, and stayed with a Russian family; secondly, my unusual mix of A levels – Maths, English, Chemistry and Art; and thirdly, I went to a normal state school and not a very good one at that. I was the only student in my year going to university. I think they felt it had been a struggle' (Debbie Friis, a sponsored student with Barclays Bank studying Maths and Psychology at Newcastle University.)

'The application form was horrendous. It must have totalled six sides and was all heavy questioning right the way from academic achievements and roles you held at school to what you thought your strengths and weaknesses were. It was like seeing yourself as an artist. They were looking for people who had done things other than study, not workaholics. I had got the Duke of Edinburgh bronze and silver awards gained for conservation projects – helping to clear up the countryside and walking expeditions done through the Scouts. That tipped it in my favour.' (David Popplewell, 19, studying Engineering at Cambridge and sponsored by ICI.)

Mike Willis, Training Officer at ICI talks about selecting students from the company's point of view.
'The first hurdle is the application form – ours is six pages long and full of searching questions. This is not admin in over-drive but intentional. Only the really committed will fill it in. Drop-out rate is around 50 per cent, which is good. We then select the best, interviewing between 40 and 50 students a year. We look for leadership qualities, team working, analytical skills and creative ability. They then attend a 2–3 day selection process which is certainly very rigorous for young people of around seventeen and a half.'

What can I expect from my interview?

Interviews vary enormously. Some companies give a full-scale assessment with psychometric testing, tricky questioning, and watching how you respond to certain situations. Others are much more laid-back and go for a straight interview. Whatever the process, if you are an A-level student it will probably be something quite new to you. Don't worry. The company will be fully aware of this and will not ask you to do something you are not capable of. Remember, too, that your competitors will be in much the same position. Still, don't expect an easy time at an interview.

THE INTERVIEW

Views on interviews from the sponsored:

'For the first round Digital came up to my University to see me. In comparison to other companies the Digital interview was very easy. There was none of that psychometric testing stuff, just a face to face interview which turned into a good old chatter. It's your personality they are after more than anything else. They look at your interests and pursuits. I am very much into pot-holing which is all about organizational skills and leadership. If you're deep under the Yorkshire Dales you've got to be able to make decisions.

The second round was at the Digital HQ in Reading. Again the interviewing was all personality – still just as friendly, still no tests – but the questioning was a lot harder and more tricky. How do you work when under stress? What do you do if you have something important on your mind, can you still apply yourself as well? Do you find it easy to make decisions when people around you are being very obstinate? They want examples. I talked of the time when hours into a climb a guy in my pot-holing team lost his nerve and wouldn't climb deeper into a cave and we couldn't go back.' (Daryl Barnes, University of Central Lancashire.)

'They had an interview day – 10 of us from schools all over the country went down to London, scary! First question – what university have you applied to. Most of the others said Oxford or Cambridge, so of course they wanted to know why I hadn't. Answer: they didn't do my course. There were tests – numerical and verbal reasoning which were quite difficult and had to be done in a very short time, plus a group exercise. Typical scenario: you are all government ministers with a budget to set and the need to argue a case for your particular ministry. Finally there was a round of interviews. Why have you applied for sponsorship with Barclays? It was a reasonable question. The truth was I wanted to explore career opportunities. I took a deep breath and that's what I said. Had I blown it? A week later I received a letter offering me a one year sponsorship which meant a £900 bursary a year and around £1,000 p.a. for eight weeks' summer vacation work. Who said honesty never pays?' (Debbie Friis)

'It was an intensive three days – interviews, psychometric testing, group activities and debates plus a trip round a plant. We even had the chance to solve a real live problem – how to clean a mixing chamber where the polymer was caking on to the side of the mixing chamber like rock. I don't think our solution was entirely practical, but our arguments were sound. At least, as the guy leading the presentation, I thought so. Certainly it was a bit stressful at times, but also great fun.' (David Popplewell)

Do I need to do a year in industry? If so, when is the best time?

Not every sponsor asks you to do a year in industry. Some just ask for vacation work. Some stipulate which year. Others leave the choice up to you. There is no right or wrong time to take a year out of academic study – just what is best for you, your sponsor, and the work you would be doing.

After A levels, some students feel that they need a break. Certainly, if you work for a company for a year before you start your degree, you will gain an insight into the career choice you are making and whether the subject is for you. It could save you three or four years heartache – many employers feel this too. If you have any doubts about the subject you are taking, then this is possibly the most sensible route.

However, some students find that if they take a break from academic study it is very difficult – if not impossible – to go back to it. And some employers feel you need to gain some academic instruction before you can benefit from the training and work experience they give.

The question of cash

Finally, if you take your year in industry at 20 you are going to earn substantially more than you would at 18. But if you take a year out at 18, the money you save will help to ease your finances once you start managing on a grant.

What do I gain from being sponsored?

● Money to supplement your grant;

● Training – most sponsorships will involve some form of training;

- Work experience;
- Guaranteed employment for the summer in an area that will assist you with your studies;
- Chance of future employment – but no guarantee;
- Help with final-year project work;
- Opportunity to gain first-hand knowledge of the working environment where you might possibly start your career.

What do I lose?

- Your holiday time is not your own;
- You would not be able to spend the whole summer abroad – going inter-railing for example;
- You have the chance to see only one industry/company during work experience;
- You make a career choice at 18 which may not be what you want at 21;
- You may be obliged to work for a company whether you want to or not, because of a payback clause;
- You may be asked to work in locations which are not very appealing and possibly a long way from home.

Comment

Some sponsors do allow their sponsored students to gain experience in other companies during vacations, as they feel that it will help to broaden their mind and knowledge. But most are loath to do so, for obvious reasons.

How much time do I have to spend with my sponsor?

Many sponsors will ask you to spend a year in industry with them, but not all. Some stipulate summer vacation work only. Barclays stipulate a minimum of eight weeks during the summer vacations. They also offer a minimum of sixteen weeks' guaranteed work during a Gap year. Of course many sponsors will offer more. Engineering firms are generally more demanding and the sponsorship is more likely to be geared to a sandwich course, so you could be looking at a full year in industry plus two summer vacation placements. One of the most flexible sponsorships we came across was BPB Paper and Packaging Ltd, who state in their sponsorship literature: 'Students are encouraged to undertake one year's work experience prior to university. This is *not* [their emphasis] compulsory.'

How will my sponsor keep in touch with me?

Methods vary – some are good; others rather haphazard. It is important to find out just how your sponsor keeps in touch with you, especially if work experience is an important element of the sponsorship. Some companies, especially if they have an input into your course, will send a representative to your university to see you each term. Tesco, for example, have close contacts with the Retail Management Course at the University of Surrey, and NatWest with the Banking courses at the University of Wales, Bangor and Loughborough University.

Planned vacation work

Other companies will hold special vacation-planning sessions. These are usually during the Easter vacation and can last anything up to a week. During these sessions you would plan with your sponsor how you want to spend your summer vacation time.

Am I obliged to join my sponsor after graduating?

You are not expected to go around cap in hand. Sponsorship is a two-way contract: both sides can expect to gain something from it. Generally, you are not obliged to join your sponsoring company after graduating, but there are exceptions to this rule, and research for this book revealed that these exceptions are increasing. Companies are definitely taking a tougher stand, and seeking value for money from their sponsorships. Some companies, for example, will stop your sponsorship payment for the final year if you don't agree to join them after graduating. Because of this, many companies will make job offers before students start their final academic year. If you turn the offer down, then the sponsorship is immediately terminated. A few companies do demand reimbursement of their sponsorship money. You would be fully informed of this before you agree to a sponsorship. All the same, our advice to those seeking sponsorship arrangement is:

● make sure any literature you are reading on sponsorship is up-to-date – school and college careers libraries are notorious for displaying last year's information;

● look at your contract in detail, and above all, check all the small print;

● question your sponsor; they will respect you for that.

Comment

The Armed Forces are slightly different from other employers; they have always included service as part of their sponsorship schemes.

REASONS GIVEN FOR THE CHANGE OF ATTITUDE AMONG SPONSORS:

● The demographic change
● The amount that is being invested in students
● Poor retention rates
● The pull of more glamorous and better-paid career areas such as finance
● The recession.

Statistical note

Latest figures show that around 50% of students join their sponsoring employer. This is 13 per cent down on the previous year's figures (IRS survey 1993). However, some companies are reporting a 100 per cent acceptance of job offers to sponsored students. As Mike Willis of ICI points out: '*Not so many good engineers are being lured by the bright lights and big money gains in the City.*'

Can my sponsor terminate my sponsorship?

Sponsorship is a legal contract. Look at the terms carefully. Most agreements will have a clause which allows the employer to withdraw if your academic performance is unsatisfactory. There may be other clauses you should watch out for.

What exactly is meant by academic performance?

If you fail the odd exam, you're probably all right, but if your end-of-year results are so bad that you have to repeat the year, then you may find that your sponsor is no longer interested.

What is a sponsorship worth to me?

Looking at it purely in cash terms, bursaries given during academic study vary from about £600 to £2,000 a year. More is an exception. There are people who give higher rates, such as the Armed Forces, but these organizations have a rather different kind of arrangement. We tried to find a meaningful average: £1,000–£1,200 p.a. was about right.

Add to this the salary you could expect to earn during a year in industry – again, this varies. We found one happy pre-university student earning £10,000 plus overtime. Salaries are generally age-related, so it depends which year you take out. A third-year student would earn considerably more than a pre-degree student. Salaries we checked out fell between £7,000 and £14,000.

You would also be paid for summer vacation work. This again is based on an age-related salary, so you should earn more in your second vacation period than in your first. Some students work the full summer vacation. Companies generally stipulate a minimum of six to eight weeks. Average pay is £715 a month (IRS survey), which over an eight-week period would be worth about £1,400.

From the employer's point of view the costs don't stop there. Generally a sponsorship includes training, which may well mean several weeks at their training centre. Some companies provide a personal tutor for students. There are also courses and meetings to arrange work experience. All this takes time, and time costs money. Every time somebody stops to tell you how to do something, it's worktime lost to the employer. Ford estimate that a sponsored student costs in excess of £15,000; British Telecom put the figure at more like £20,000 (based on figures given by employers for students joining them in 1991).

How do I choose a sponsor?

Asked what was the best way to choose a sponsor, one student said: '*If he covers your subject, be practical – go for the cash.*' Certainly cash is something to be borne in mind, but there are many factors to take into consideration even when you're looking at the money:

1 Compare salaries and bursaries: the plus of one might rule out the minus of another. Ford, for example, offer a fairly low bursary starting at around £600, but their monthly salary ranges from £871 in the first year to £1,308 in the fourth.

2 Training and work experience: this must be the real deciding factor. How you spend your time in industry could make all the difference to your degree results, and so to your future career.

- Check out the training schemes. Engineers who will eventually be seeking chartered status should ensure that the training they get is recognized by the appropriate institution.

- Check what you will be doing during working periods: whether you are just an extra pair of hands, or on a well-organized programme of development. Companies with sponsorship experience, and therefore well tried and tested sponsorship schemes, may be the best bet.

- Talk to other students on the scheme; what looks good on paper may not work out so well in practice.

- Find out what projects have been undertaken by sponsored students in the past.

- Check how many sponsored students join the company as graduates.

3 Ask yourself: is this the sort of company where I would want to make my career? A sponsorship puts you in a good position for eventual employment.

4 Geographical location: if you are a Northerner born and bred, think twice before joining a company that operates only in the South, or vice versa. Your industrial placements will be spent on your sponsor's premises, and that might not be in your home town. Perhaps that could be fun for a year, but is it where you would want to work after qualifying?

5 Accommodation and travel: if you have to stay away from home during work periods, will your sponsor help with accommodation costs and travel? If they won't, that could eat into your salary.
6 Work abroad: occasionally some companies – Ford, Arthur Andersen, Barclays, ICI for example – offer work experience abroad for summer vacation placements to a few sponsored students.
7 Outsider or employee: some companies treat their sponsored students as employees, giving them many of the same benefits – e.g. 22½ per cent off the price of a car at Ford.
8 Check for a payback clause in case you don't join your sponsor when you graduate. Check also if sponsored students are dropped from the scheme if they don't agree to join the company in their final year.

Comment: That year's industrial training – An exciting adventure or a time of loneliness?

At school, and then at college, you are surrounded by people of your own age, people who want to do the same things as you. Friends are easily found. This may not be the case once you are at work. It is always exciting to go to new places and have new experiences, but if your work placement means being away from home, it's worth finding out where you will be staying, who you will be with, how often you will get home and what there is to do in the evenings. Most companies are well aware of the problems of slotting young people into a new environment and have contingency plans, but not all.

When should I apply for sponsorship?

Full degree course sponsorship: Some companies offer sponsorship for your full degree course. Applications for these schemes should be made early in your final school year, and at least by the time you send in your UCAS form.

Second-year degree course sponsorship: Some sponsors like to see commitment to their course among students before offering sponsorship.

Final-year degree course sponsorship: Increasingly, employers are offering sponsorship to students for just the final year of their degree course. Often this will be offered after a successful industrial placement year, or a summer vacation period. Employers offering sponsorship at this stage will expect students to agree to join them after graduation.

What's the competition for sponsorship?

Phenomenal. All sponsors say that applications outstrip sponsorships available, and it is getting worse – so get in early. The earlier you apply, the better. Applications for full course sponsorship should have been made by the time you send in your UCAS form.

How many companies should I apply to?

Students we asked thought around ten applications, but we did hear of people applying to over twenty companies.

What is a sandwich course?

A sandwich course is primarily an academic training which includes within it an element of practical training in industry. The sandwich can be made up in a variety of ways – described as either thick or thin sandwiches.

A thick or a thin sandwich – which is best?

The thick sandwich is generally four years with one year – generally the third – spent in industry. But it can be a five-year course with two years on a degree course, one year in industry, a final year back on the degree course and a further year in industry. Yet another five-year option is the 1.3.1 package, which offers one year in industry, three on a degree course, and the final year back in industry. This is rather less integrated into your degree course. The thin sandwich will most probably be a four-year course with alternate six-month periods spent in industry and education. Often a pre-degree industrial year is taken. Courses at Brunel are organized on this basis.

Which is best? That depends on how you like to work. Some people like the idea of their academic study being well integrated into their practical work. Others find the interruptions of practical work disrupting.

What is a sponsor looking for?

A straw poll amongst sponsors suggested that sponsors favour students with:

● good A-level grades
● maturity

- potential
- ambition
- evident team skills
- a sense of humour
- a hard-working attitude
- the ability to get a good second-class degree
- interest in their degree topic
- ability to assimilate information and learn quickly.

What if I'm turned down for sponsorship?

Don't get disheartened if you get turned down by them all. Remember: there are an increasing number of students chasing a decreasing number of sponsorships, and the picture is changing all the time. You can always try again. Check out the section in Chapter 4 on getting work experience.

Which comes first – UCAS or sponsorship?

They both come at once, which makes for complications. However, they are aware of this, so a system has been worked out.

First you should discover whether a sponsor you are interested in requires you to gain a place on a particular course – if so, you should name that course on your UCAS form.

However, it could happen that an employer you had not originally been very interested in offers you a sponsorship with the proviso that you gain a place on a course not named in your selection on your application form. While UCAS do not generally allow students to make alterations to their original application, in the case of sponsorship they usually relax this rule.

Deferred Entry?

Another complication is whether you want deferred entry or not. If you get sponsorship, your sponsor may require you to do a pre-degree year in industry, but at application time you may not know this. If in doubt, apply for the current year. It is always easier to ask a university to defer your entry rather than bring it forward. On some courses, especially popular courses such as Law, deferment may be more difficult to arrange.

People who can help you to get sponsorship

If you haven't been able to arrange sponsorship or work experience for yourself, THE YEAR IN INDUSTRY might be able to help you. Full details of this organization, and the address to write to, are given in Chapter 4.

Am I guaranteed a job at the end of a sponsorship?

No. Employers are under no obligation to offer you a job and are unlikely to promise you one when they agree to sponsor you, so don't bank on it. Their intention in sponsoring you is eventual employment, but there are many reasons why things don't quite work out as planned – for example:

● there is a recession;

● the company's plans change and the area of work you are involved in disappears;

● you do not come up to expectations;

● your own career ideas have changed.

Employers invest a great deal of time, energy and money in sponsoring a student, and they are loath to let that investment go to waste.

Will my university find me sponsorship?

If you are accepted on to a course either conditionally or uncon-ditionally, it is always a good idea to ask the course director if they know of any sponsoring companies. Often they will have a list. Some students will find that they are automatically offered sponsors to apply to, and on some courses where employers actually sponsor the course – such as the Retail Management course at Surrey University – the course sponsors are involved in the selection procedure. College prospectuses may give you some guidance.

Warwick undergraduates or prospective undergraduates of the University can contact the Student Sponsorship Office set up in November 1990. The Office has a large database of information on sponsorship schemes, covering a wide range of subject areas. For further information, contact: The Student Sponsorship Offices, The University of Warwick, Coventry CV4 7AL Tel: 0203 523523.

Who to contact

Your university or college may well have a list of sponsors who are interested in sponsoring students on your particular course.

What to read

- *Sponsorship for Students*: this lists over 50 companies, industrial organizations and funding bodies that can provide sponsorships. It is published annually by COIC (Careers and Occupational Information Centre) in conjunction with Hobsons Publishing plc., and is available from your local careers advice centre or COIC PO Box 348, Bristol BS99 7FE.

- *Everything You Wanted to Know about Sponsorship*, published by Amoeba Publications, Lakeside Manor Farm, Crowland Road, Eye Green, Cambridge PE6 7TT. Tel: 0733 223113.

- *Sponsorship and Training Opportunities in Engineering*, published by the Institution of Mechanical Engineers on behalf of the engineering profession. It lists around 59 sponsors and is available free from The Institution of Mechanical Engineers, Northgate Avenue, Bury St Edmunds, Suffolk IP32 6BN. Tel: 0284 763277.

Not all sponsors advertise

If you look down the list of sponsors in most sponsorship books, you will be surprised how many large companies appear not to offer sponsorship or work experience, yet do. Many companies, such as IBM, just don't have to bother to advertise – the requests flood in anyway. They are so inundated with applicants that they have more than they can handle. To reduce applications and the need to advertise, other companies will have special relationships with selected schools or universities. So just because a company doesn't advertise sponsorship, that shouldn't stop you from asking. A well-phrased letter may do you some good, and it can never do you any harm. After all, any company should be pleased that you are interested in them. You might even find that your application jogs them into doing something. That's what happened to David Stephens when he wrote to Arthur Andersen.

'After my A levels I wanted to break from academic study; I also wanted to travel. But to do that, I needed some money. I wrote to a number of accountancy firms. Arthur Andersen offered me the best deal.

I would join the new intake of graduates, do the same training, gain the same auditing experience, earn the same money, but work for only six months. I wanted to cram as much as I could into that Gap year. Arthur Andersen understood.

The first six weeks were spent in training, which included two weeks in Segovia in Spain. The next four months I worked with the Industrial and Commerical Audit Group, spending most of my time with five or six large clients. That's the interesting thing about accountancy work – you're always out working in other people's businesses, dipping into what they are doing. And don't believe what they say about auditing – I found it fascinating. I even got involved in a takeover bid.

Arthur Andersen had no sponsoring scheme at the time, but I wanted to continue the relationship, so suggested they considered sponsoring me through university. They hummed and hawed and then agreed.

Arthur Andersen confirmed that their scheme had evolved rather than been a conscious decision to fill a need. Six years ago, four A-level students wrote to them asking for work experience during a pre-university year, David was one of them. They proved to be first-class students and the firm soon realised this was an excellent way of attracting high-fliers at an early stage. The following year they took on another five students and the next year extended the scheme to thirty-five. By the following year they were looking for 50 – and so it snowballed.

Don't forget the smaller companies

If you're thinking in terms of your CV, then it must be admitted that a well-known name will carry more weight than a smaller company. A big company that is used to taking on sponsored students may be better organized and give you better experience and training, but this is not necessarily so. Less well-known companies, and newcomers to sponsorship, don't attract the same number of applicants as the big names, so there's less competition.

Will sponsorship be good for my CV?

Yes – but with reservations. Seventy-three per cent of the companies we asked said sponsorship was a plus point. The others felt that it made little difference. James Davidson, Careers Adviser at Bath University, said that while sponsorship on your CV shows that you have been 'selected', it was the work experience that would be seen as the important element on a CV.

Of course employers will probably ask why you didn't join the company that sponsored you, so you will need to have a well-phrased answer. Most employers realize that a decision made at the age of 18 may not look so right when you are 22. It's always worth remembering that your would-be new employer may write to your sponsor for a reference, so it's important to leave your sponsoring company on good terms.

Is it best to apply to local companies?

It is always best to apply to a company that interests you. Nevertheless, some companies do prefer to take on local people. From their point of view, there is no accommodation problem when it comes to work experience, and statistics show that many students want to return to their own home town to work when they complete their studies. So the company is more likely to keep the sponsored student as an employee.

Is sponsorship always the best idea?

Generally, sponsoring companies will want you to undertake all your industrial placement and work experience with them. While this often means that your work periods are better planned, it can also mean that the experience you gain is restricted to a specific area or work environment, and only one company. This could limit your view and outlook. As you can see, there are pluses and minuses on both sides. A company that is prepared to move you around its different departments and sites has a great deal to offer.

Can I get sponsorship once I've started my degree?

Yes. As we said in answer to 'When should I apply for sponsorship', more and more companies are giving sponsorship just for the final year or from the second year of a course. These sponsorships often develop from a successful period of work experience during the summer vacations, or through an industrial placement during a sandwich course. Marks and Spencer, for example, are typical: they offer sponsorship for the final year only to students who are accepted on to their graduate training scheme after a period of work experience. Unilever have recently changed their scheme for engineers, reducing the number of full-degree-sponsored students from ten to four and creating twenty-eight final-year sponsorships. Some students prefer to wait until they have some idea of the direction in which their studies are going before they commit themselves to an employer.

Advice note

Been unlucky in securing sponsorship? Try the back-door entry. When you're looking for a summer vacation job, seek out companies that you feel could be interested in sponsoring your particular skills. You may be lucky, there's no harm in asking.

Should sponsorship determine which course I choose?

In theory no. First you should decide on the course that best suits you. You're going to spend at least three solid years and possibly more studying, so make sure you're going to enjoy it, otherwise the results could be at best disappointing and at worst disastrous. It's no good studying Paper Science because some of the most lucrative sponsorships are given for this area, if you're really interested in History or Hotel Management. However, if you are particularly interested in gaining work experience in a certain company, or there are several courses you are interested in, and by opting for one it could lead to sponsorship, then obviously sponsorship should influence your choice.

I'm a sponsored student, but find I don't like the course I'm studying. What can I do?

This happens. You choose a course in something that perhaps you have never studied before, and after a term or so you discover that you and the subject just don't get along together. A sponsorship is not a life sentence, neither is a degree course. Talk first to your college tutor. It may be just one aspect of the course you don't like. Then talk to your sponsor. You will probably be able to change your degree course, but it may be more difficult – or impossible – for your sponsor to put you on an appropriate sponsorship scheme. Don't despair. If they were sufficiently impressed by you to give you a sponsorship in the first place, they may well be able to accommodate your needs. Otherwise, you may just have to part company. Whatever you do, be frank and

---

FACT CHECK

Average starting salary paid to a 21-year-old graduate with a second-class Honours degree in 1993 was £13,004 p.a.

Law practices pay graduates the highest starting salaries in the UK: £17,000 p.a. (1993 average figure).

1,647 graduates – that's 12 per cent of all graduates recruited in 1991 – had been sponsored in their final academic year.

184,000 students – a record number – are expected to graduate from higher education institutions in the UK in 1994. The greatest increase will be from the new universities.

It is estimated that 50 per cent of sponsored students start their working careers with their sponsor.

Over 450 firms in the UK are thought to offer sponsorships.

153,753 students in the UK are enrolled on sandwich courses.

---

up-front about your change of heart – and the sooner the better, before too much time and money are wasted.

Here two sponsored students talk about their experiences.

Sponsorship with ICI

Sponsored students at ICI spend a period of pre-university industrial training of between 2–12 months with ICI – the length of training is the student's choice. This is followed by eight-week vacation placements in the summer. They are paid during the work placements and receive a bursary of £1350 during each academic year.

David Popplewell, 19, now in his first year of an Engineering degree at Cambridge, talks about his sponsorship with ICI.

'I decided to spend a full year with ICI before starting my degree. It was the best decision I could have made. The year was minutely planned from beginning to end.

The first three months were at a training school near Liverpool getting practical experience in things like metal bashing, lathing, welding – all new to me, while also keeping up with the theoretical side – advanced maths and computing. We were all sponsored students living together which was fun.

I moved to the ICI plant near Middlesbrough to shadow workers and managers on the shop floor, but found it was very hands on. Then came my first chance to tackle a real problem: a furnace kept going out and they wanted to know why. It was nice to think I was doing something of consequence.

My second project was to design a fruit and vegetable peeler for the disabled. It took three weeks to design, four weeks to construct, was a foot high and packed with so much electronics it needed an expert to keep it going. Hardly your handy home Moulinex, but . . . I felt I had learnt a tremendous amount, not least that maths doesn't solve every problem.

There were visits to other companies to see how they operate, a week's 'outward-bound' type course to challenge our leadership and team-work skills, and two weeks training in Germany where we learnt as much about the efficiency of their social life as we did their industrial operations. Lasting memories include bike rides across the Dutch border to Amsterdam and deep discussions on the drug problems. The ICI idea is to broaden your experience, and not just push you into the ICI mould.

Pay during my year out and my sponsorship bursary means I am not facing the financial problems of other students or the worry of finding holiday work, which next summer I hope will be in the States – sponsored by ICI but not necessarily with an ICI company – see what I mean about broadening your experience.'

Sponsorship with Midland Bank

Dave Hollins, 21, is studying Banking and Finance at Loughborough University. He is currently on a year's work experience with the Midland which will lead to final year sponsorship and a job offer. Pay during work placement is £8750. Bursary £1000 p.a.

'Selection for sponsorship was quite daunting as you went on the same assessment centre as the graduates, some of whom were 3–4 years older than me. It was an intensive day crammed with interviews and group tests. One was to set out the business case for a new toy which we then built in straws. Another was to get from one deserted island to another without falling prey to the sharks – I survived!

I had already been offered a year's work experience with Mobil Oil at a salary of £14,000 – £5,250 more than with Midland. As an impoverished student it was very tempting, but . . .

I had worked for the Midland Bank before, during a vacation, and I enjoyed it. The people were friendly and the deal would include sponsorship for my final year worth £1,000, and a job offer when I qualified.

There were also other advantages from Midland, like the use of an extensive library, work related to my degree, a mentor to advise me, time to study for and take my AC AIB banking exams, and four placements in different parts of the country (the Mobil offer was just in London). When you take all that into consideration, when you read the small print, it really wasn't such a difficult decision.

Midland's year in industry is well planned. For the first 3 months I returned to the Stoke-on-Trent branch where I had worked before. That was fun. I was returning to friends, and I could get down to work right away. The object of the placement was to see how a branch operated so I moved round all the departments at break neck speed. I have now moved to the Mortgage Service Centre in Sheffield where I am processing mortgages for customers.

My next placement will be with First Direct, their telephone banking service centre in Leeds. And then four months in something like risk management, marketing or finance.

Probably the most important thing I've learnt so far is how to organize my time. At University you can plan your study over a ten week stretch, but here the phone rings, you drop everything, cope, and then reorganize your time.

I've always managed to find a vacation job and now with the sponsorship I expect to graduate without any debt.

Yes, I would like a career with the Midland, and no, I'm not just saying that because I'm on their sponsorship scheme – I chose them remember. As part of the Hong Kong and Shanghai group Midland have got a lot of potential, and a global outlook.'

4
PAYING YOUR WAY

Work experience, working abroad, a year out, travel

There are many reasons why students work, either before or during their study course. In this chapter we investigate some of those reasons and give advice on what sort of work you can expect to find; how to go about getting it; whom to contact and what to read. There is also some helpful information on the travel scene, insurance and holidaying abroad, and anecdotes from students about their experiences.

SEVEN REASONS WHY STUDENTS WORK

Reason 1: to make money

A recent survey among students showed that a clear majority work from sheer financial necessity, and the aim is to earn as much as possible:

84 per cent worked during vacations.
12.5 per cent worked at weekends.
12.5 per cent worked in the evenings.
5 per cent worked weekends, evenings and vacations.

FAST FACTS ON WORK

Why do students work?

- For money
- For experience
- To travel
- To fill in a Gap year

Where do they work?

- In shops
- In restaurants
- In pubs
- In camps in America
- On a kibbutz
- In teaching

How much do they earn?

£115–£175 p.w. on average.

We didn't ask for their final degree grades.

While tutors may frown and wonder about the effect working, especially during term time, may have on your studies, what could be more depressing – or, indeed, wasteful of opportunity – than to find you haven't sufficient funds to take part in college activities, buy your books or, indeed, benefit from the occasional trip abroad?

Most students want or need to take jobs during the long summer vacations, and an increasing number are taking a year out between A levels and starting to study for their degree. While the motivation for deferred entry is more likely to be the need to 'get off the academic treadmill' (see page 98), in retrospect many students feel that the money they managed to save during that Gap year has put them on a sound financial footing and saved them from colossal anxiety in their first year.

If your aim is to save money, then your best bet is to work as close to home as possible, where bed and board are likely to be at a very advantageous rate – if not free – and avoid travel.

In these recessionary times jobs aren't easy to come by, especially for six to nine months, and vacation jobs are even harder to find. But with a little enterprise, some initiative and plenty of pen and leg work, you should succeed.

● Try employers whose workforce includes women with young children, who tend to give up work during the school holidays – shops, supermarkets, restaurants.

● Try to find an employer with a recurring need, so that you can come back next year. McDonald's like to have a team of students they can call on during the summer vacations.

● If you've got a skill – typing, shorthand, word-processing, driving, computer knowledge – it could be easier.

Students seeking evening or weekend work during term time will probably find it easier in a large city than in a small town. London students should fare better than most – which is just as well, since they are amongst the most financially stretched.

You are most likely to find work in: bars, restaurants or general catering, dispatch-riding (must have own wheels and a fearless mentality!), pizza delivery, office or domestic cleaning, childminding, market research, modelling, offices (temporary), shops, hotels.

Who to contact

● employment agencies
● job centres
● local employers on spec.

What to read

● Local newspaper job ads
● *Summer Jobs in Britain*
● *Teenager's Vacation Guide*

These two books are available from Vacation Work, 9 Park End Street, Oxford OX1 1HJ. Tel: 0865 241978

Reason 2: to get sponsorship

Many companies like to test people out before they offer sponsorship: National Power, Nuclear Electric, Marks and Spencer, and Digital operate this system. Often they will offer work experience during the summer vacation, or as an industrial placement either before starting your degree course or as part of a sandwich course. If they like you, they may well offer sponsorship for the whole or the rest of your degree course. There is no guarantee, of course, that the placement will bear fruit. The course director at your institution may well have a list of suitable companies interested in your particular discipline; otherwise it's a matter of writing round. Many companies don't advertise work experience because they are inundated with applications. Start with local employers. Living away from home, even if your employer helps with expenses, will eat into your earnings.

Who to contact

● THE YEAR IN INDUSTRY – see section 'Name to know', p. 101.

● Local employers that interest you – many employers prefer to sponsor local students. Don't forget the smaller companies. Some may never have thought of offering work experience before, so it can be a matter of making yourself sound useful.

● Your course director.

What to read

● *Sponsorship and Training Opportunities in Engineering*, free from The Institution of Mechanical Engineers, Northgate Avenue, Bury St Edmunds, Suffolk IP32 6BN. Tel: 0284 763277

● *Sponsorship for Students*, from your local careers advice centre or COIC, PO Box 348, Bristol BS99 7FE.

● *Everything you Wanted to Know about Sponsorship*, published by Amoeba Publications, Lakeside Manor Farm, Crowland Road, Eye Green, Cambridge PE6 7TT. Tel: 0733 223113

Reason 3: vacation work experience

Many students use vacations as a time to gain some work experience in an area that will help them with their degree, or with entrance into a career. Many organizations which are unable to offer sponsorship or industrial placement do offer vacation-work experience – banks, insurance companies, accountancy and law firms, for example.

You may also find openings into areas where sponsorship is impossible and industrial placements are difficult to find, such as personnel, marketing or publishing. If you are considering the media, advertising or journalism, you'll probably find it's MISSION IM-POSSIBLE. You could try some of the local radio stations, but it'll probably be unpaid work.

Work experience placements are not all one sided, the employer gets something out of it too. But getting one is incredibly competitive.

'There has been a growing tendency to view vacation placements as an essential element of the recruitment process, but this is misconceived', says Chris Perrin, partner with responsibility for all graduate recruitment and training at international law firm Clifford Chance. *'The real value of vacation placements is to give students the chance to be sure they are aiming for the right career; that many law firms have used them as part of the recruitment process simply highlights the fact that they feel happier recruiting from the vacation schemes than otherwise – i.e. their selection process for training contracts is not sufficiently exhaustive. We recruit about 90 graduates a year, but only about 20–25 of them have been in our vacation schemes, and they have to go through all the interviews and assessment exercises along with other candidates we have not seen on vacation schemes. Vacation schemes are therefore an excellent experience, but are not an automatic ticket to a training contract if the firm's selection process is exhaustive'*. (Clifford Chance currently pays £155 a week for a 2 or 3 week placement, at Easter or in the Summer).

Who to contact

● Local employers
● Course directors
● College noticeboards
● Your college careers advisers.

Oxford University Careers Office runs a special scheme called Vac Train, which seeks out employers willing to take on pre-final-year undergraduates for 6–12 weeks during the summer vacation. Currently they have 44 companies on their books, and last summer they placed 108 students. When first introduced they believed their scheme was unique, but other institutions may well have similar schemes – it's worth checking.

Reason 4: to get off the academic treadmill

Taking a year out after A levels – a 'Gap' year, as it is generally called – is becoming increasingly popular. After at least thirteen solid years on the academic treadmill, many young people just feel that they need a chance to recharge their batteries. Most universities will accept deferred entry; many institutions – such as Oxford and Cambridge – actively encourage it. But don't assume that deferred entry is an automatic right. You must always ask, and if the course is popular, it may be refused.

Many young people use this time to gain a skill or experience in a specific organization as well as making money, so that they have a ready-made job to walk into during vacations, once they have started their degree course.

Who to contact

- Banks, insurance companies, accountancy firms – many do offer work experience; always worth a try.
- Shops, supermarkets, chain stores – try to find an organization with a number of local outlets, and one which offers a training scheme.
- Teaching – you don't actually need any training to take up a temporary position as assistant teacher or matron in a preparatory school. As an assistant matron you could find yourself darning socks and getting the kids up in the morning. As an assistant teacher you'd probably be involved in organizing sport and out-of-school activities, coaching, supervising prep and classes when staff were away. Current rate is around £75 p.w., with everything – food, accommodation – found. Term ends in July, so you would then have two months' travelling time. Try Gabbitas, Truman and Thring, 6–8 Sackville Street, Piccadilly, London W1X 2BR. Tel: 071–734 0161.
- Archaeological digs: it won't earn you a fortune – more likely nothing; subsistence pay is given only occasionally – but it can be fascinating work. See *The British Archaeological News*, published by the Council for British Archaeology, Bowes Morrell House, 111 Walmgate, York YO1 2UA Tel: 0904 671417, every other month – subscription £9.50 for students, but should be available in public libraries. See also BTCV details under section on voluntary work.
- THE YEAR IN INDUSTRY – see 'Name to know', page 101.

What to read

- *Taking a Year Off*, published by Trotman & Co., 12 Hill Rise, Richmond TW10 6UA.

- *A Year Off. . . A Year On?* – Hobsons, Bateman Street, Cambridge CB2 1BR.

- *Jobs Before Cambridge*, issued by the Cambridge University Careers Service, Stuart House, Mill Lane, Cambridge, CB2 1YE or from colleges.

- *Jobs in the 'Gap' Year*, available only from the Independent Schools Careers Organization, 12a–18a Princess Way, Camberley, Surrey GU15 3SP.

- *Working Holidays* – try grape-picking, yacht crewing, driving, tour-guiding, beekeeping – there's information on 99,000 jobs in 99 different countries. Available from the Central Bureau, Seymour Mews House, Seymour Mews, London W1H 9PE.

'As it was a well-trained prep school, the first time I stepped into the classroom they all stood up. It's daunting to be faced with twenty 12-year-olds when you are only just 18 and just out of school yourself. I was so nervous the only word that came out was SIT. They gave me some funny looks, but thought I was very strict, which certainly helped later on. I was there to teach Biology and Chemistry. I enjoyed it enormously and will probably return to teaching when I've finished my PhD.' (Mark, Durham University)

Reason 5: as an industrial placement

The idea of the four-year sandwich course which included an industrial placement was never envisaged as a financial life-saver, but many students are finding that a year in industry, with a good salary, is helping them to clear their debts, while they gain invaluable experience. But with more higher education institutions developing more sandwich courses, finding good industrial placements is becoming increasingly difficult. This is felt mostly where courses are fairly new and the institutions haven't yet built up a good rapport with industrial concerns.

In the beginning, industrial placements were largely for students on Engineering courses, but increasingly, Business Studies courses, Retail courses, Computer courses and many others include an industrial placement year.

The University of Wales, Aberystwyth has pioneered a new initiative to give any student within the university who is not already on a

NAME TO KNOW: THE YEAR IN INDUSTRY

If you are looking for experience in industry, THE YEAR IN INDUSTRY can help.

The organization has extensive contacts with companies in industry which are interested in taking on A-level and BTEC students for a year's work before a degree course. In the first instance, it operates more as a clearing house, similar to UCAS, with twenty regional organisers based at universities throughout the country. Last year over 220 companies took part in the scheme. The scheme involves a training element, which takes the form of a series of workshops and seminars covering practical skills and aspects of work of general interest such as communication, finance, marketing and design. This training is in addition to any training your employer provides. The training is paid for by your employer and includes a short term special project and a public project presentation. Year in Industry training can count towards accreditation by professional institutions.

THE YEAR IN INDUSTRY lay down a minimum salary that companies must pay students. Most companies pay more. Most students placed by them are given sponsorship for their degree.

Who to contact: Students start applying in the September of their final A-level year. The earlier you get in, the better. Interviews with companies are generally held the following January to May. Your school or college should have details of your Regional Year in Industry Director. If not, contact Brian L. Tripp, National Director Year in Industry, Simon Buildings, University of Manchester, Oxford Road, Manchester M13 9PL. Tel: 061–275 4396.

Satisfied students say:

'I would recommend the scheme very strongly, the experience it gives you is invaluable.' Mark Powell – John Laing Construction – Loughborough

'Very useful insight into what can be expected when taking a career in industry. A breather from education and a way to ensure you have made the right choice of University course.' Bruce Boutell – Bierrum and Partners – Bristol

'It's definitely worth doing. I feel I have developed a lot, learnt a lot about working for a big company and the working world in general.' Sarah Monk – ICI Bioproducts – Oxford

'I have learnt a great deal in this year in industry and think that it will give me an advantage over students who have just come from school when starting in university.' Richard Morris – Civil Engineering Contractors – Swansea

sandwich course the opportunity to take an industrial year out. The scheme is called YES (Year in Employment Scheme), and currently between 40 and 70 students at Aberystwyth are saying YES to the opportunity. They come from a range of disciplines: Arts, Economics and Social Science, Information and Library Studies, Law, Rural Science and Science. You can choose a placement that is relevant to your degree subject, such as accounting, marketing and scientific research – these are the most popular – or use the time to experience work in an area that is totally new to you such as personnel management, journalism, or production management. You can even work abroad: YES students are currently in the USA, Australia, Bahrain, Egypt, Guyana, Tanzania and Switzerland. The scheme has been going for some fifteen years, and Aberystwyth is adamant – with some justification – that the skills learnt during the year out have enhanced both degree performance and employment prospects. The latest figures they print show that 70 per cent of YES graduates were awarded a 2:1 or first-class degree, compared with 43 per cent for the total graduating from the University College of Wales, Aberystwyth for that year. Many students return to college with definite job offers, sponsorship, and even contracts sewn up.

A must for anyone considering taking a sandwich course but not sure what's on offer is the Directory published annually by the Association for Sandwich Education and Training (ASET for short). This lists most of the Sandwich Courses currently being offered by Universities and Colleges of Further and Higher Education in the UK – over 1,000 different courses in all. The directory gives listings under both subject headings and institutions, along with addresses and contact names and has a useful subject index.

Letter home

Richard Arnett, who is reading Aquatic Biology at the University of Wales, Aberystwyth, decided to take advantage of the University's Year in Employment Scheme and undertook a project in Australia on large sea mammals because he felt work experience would make him more competitive when seeking a job. Opposite, he tells of his experiences.

* Since returning Richard has presented a paper on his research at an international symposium in Texas. See also Andrew's letter on page 120.

Aberystwyth, Dyfed
October

G'day folks

I expected to enjoy my time upside down in Australia, but not half as much as I actually did. A five month job quickly turned into a 15 month stay terminated only by my need to return for my final year.

I was studying whales and dolphins with a team from Sydney University, a project which took me along the coasts of Queensland, New South Wales, Victoria, South Australia and Western Australia. The concept of distance is very different over there; we thought nothing of making a three-day coach trip between study sites – journeys which traversed some of the most contrasting and arguably most beautiful country that I have ever seen.

It didn't take me very long to get into the Australian way of life. Within a month I had stopped wearing shoes and bought my first surf-board. Surfing was the first of many new experiences I had in Australia. Edited highlights include swimming with whales and dolphins, being chased by sharks and snakes and getting bitten by spiders.

When I wasn't working in the field and playing with the wild life, I was living in Sydney and working at the university analysing the data I had collected. There I met a lot of people, though very few were Australian. I shared a flat with a Bosnian refugee and a South African student.

Back now in Aberystwyth, I can't wait to graduate and go off chasing the whales and dolphins once again.

Hang ten

Richard

Who to ask

● If you are not a sponsored student, contact your department at your university. They will have a list of possible employers.

● Contact employers direct – don't forget that smaller companies which might offer just one placement often don't get deluged.

What to Read

● Check out publications listed under 'Reason 2', page 97.

● *ASET Directory of Sandwich Courses*, available from the ASET Secretary, Sheffield Hallam University, Pond Street, Sheffield S1 1WB. Tel: 0742 532517

Reason 6: to travel abroad

What employer is going to give you three months off every nine months, or say 'Take a year off and see the world'? None. You will never, ever get holidays as long as this again. So if you have a yen to travel, make the most of your time and budget wisely.

When you start to investigate the student travel scene, you'll discover that there's plenty of help available. The path to the Continent, the kibbutz or Camp America is well worn. There is a plethora of publications and organizations, cheap travel firms, ticket concessions – even government advice handed out to get you safely there and back. If that makes it all sound rather overplayed, pioneers can always be accommodated. Backpacking and inter-railing are always journeys into the unknown. Things rarely turn out exactly as you had envisaged.

If it's a job you're interested in, try skiing instructor, courier, au pair, grape-picker, children's summer camp assistant, archaeological digger.

Who to contact

● AIESEC, the International Exchange Programme, puts students and recently qualified graduates in touch with companies throughout the world which are offering work experience for a vacation or longer placement. It operates in 78 countries and has a membership of over 60,000 students and graduates. AIESEC is represented at 32 universities throughout the UK. Check with your institution to see if it has a branch, otherwise contact AIESEC, United Kingdom, 26 Phipp Street, London EC2A 4NR. Tel: 071–366 7939.

- To work in the USA, Canada, Jamaica, Malta or Australia, start with BUNAC (British Universities North America Club). They organize three work programmes:

BUNACAMP finds students jobs working with children in summer camps, helping to look after them and arranging activities. Some experience of working with children is required.

KAMP finds students jobs in the kitchen or maintenance/general areas of children's summer camps. No experience is required.

Work America Programme enables students to take jobs anywhere in the USA. There are similar schemes covering Australia, Canada, Jamaica and Malta.

To meet the cash crisis facing many students, BUNAC have set up a helpful financial help scheme, which provides interest-free air-fare loans so you can borrow enough to get yourself there, and then pay it back gradually through your earnings. Those working on the BUNACAMP and KAMP programmes will find that their air fares are paid.

All enquiries: BUNAC, 16 Bowling Green Lane, London EC1R 0BD. Tel: 071–251 3472.

Try also Camp America, which recruits students to work in children's summer camps: Dept YO, 37a Queens Gate, London SW7 5HR Tel: 071–581 7373.

● Work on a kibbutz can be fun. You may have to pay for your own travel, but not for living expenses. Contact Kibbutz Representatives, 1a Accommodation Road, London NW11 8ED. Tel: 081–458 9235; or Project 67, 10 Hatton Garden, London EC1N 8AH. Tel: 071–831 7626.

● Au pair/nanny: Try adverts in *The Lady* magazine and *The Times*; also the *Au Pair and Nanny's Guide to Working Abroad*, from Vacation Work, 9 Park End Street, Oxford OX1 1HJ. Tel: 0865 241978.

● GAP Activity Projects Ltd arranges work to fill the Gap year between A levels and higher education. It has schemes in 28 countries including Australia, the Falklands, France, Germany, India, Israel, Mexico, Nepal, New Zealand, Pakistan, South America and the USA. Contact them at 44 Queen's Road, Reading, Berkshire RG1 4BB. Tel: 0734 594914. Office open 9.30–4.30 Monday to Friday. For information send a large SAE (34p stamp)

● Courier – many travel companies will employ young people, especially those with languages, as couriers.

We have mentioned just a few of the opportunities available abroad to whet your appetite – there are many more. The list of books and directories available to help you make a considered decision is exhaustive. We have limited our reading list to those books which are free or probably within your price range, or those you are most likely to find in your local library.

What to read

● *Working Holidays*, published by the Central Bureau of Educational Visits and Exchanges – usually available in libraries, from any good bookshop, or the Bureau itself at Seymour Mews House, Seymour Mews, London W1H 9PE. Tel: 071–486 5101.

● *Summer Jobs USA 1994*, published by Vacation Work, 9 Park End Street, Oxford OX1 1HJ.

● *Summer Jobs Abroad*, published by Vacation Work (address above).

● *Live and Work in France . . . in Spain and Portugal . . . in Italy . . . in Germany . . . in Belgium and the Netherlands and Luxembourg* – a series of books giving details of temporary and permanent work in various countries. Prices vary. From Vacation Work.

● *Working Your Way Around the World* – offers authoritative advice on how to find work as you travel, with hundreds of first-hand accounts. Find out how to become a barmaid, kiwifruit packer, ski guide or jackaroo: also from Vacation Work.

● *Working in Ski Resorts* – offers details on a variety of jobs from au pair to disc jockey and snow-cleaner: from Vacation Work.

● *Teaching English Abroad* – guide to short- and long-term opportunities for both trained and untrained. Eastern Europe, Greece, Turkey, Japan – the choice is vast and varied: from Vacation Work.

● *Directory of Jobs Careers Abroad*, from Vacation Work.

'Students have the time and the opportunity to travel and experience the "ideal" of freedom. You won't get that chance again.' (Roger, Loughborough University, back from Africa)

On the travel trail

Jo, now a first year student at Nottingham Trent University and her friend Sophie, a history student at Edinburgh University, decided to take a year off after A-levels and travel to South East Asia and India. For Sophie, financing the trip meant four months working 9–5 in an insurance office plus three evening shifts a week in a pub as a bar-maid and two shifts in *Pizza Express* – total earnings £2,700. Jo, who already had some savings, worked in a school for autistic children aged 3–16 for three months. By January they were ready to go on their travels. These extracts from Jo's diary will give you some idea of their experiences on that 'incredible' five month journey.

Jan 27, Bali
Arrived late after interminable plane journey. Staying in cottage – twin room £8 a night. Complete black-out due to bad storms knocking out electricity. Whole place looks very authentic by candle light. Hope it looks as good tomorrow.

Jan 28, Bali
Continually hassled by sellers and beggars – I suppose we're going to have to get used to that.

Jan 31, Senggigi, Lombok

Nightmare ferry journey due to previous night's celebrations with friends. Island quite beautiful and off the tourist route. Drinks in bar served to you cross-legged on cushions. Taught backgammon and card tricks by friendly local Indonesians while guitars softly played – truly a mellow atmosphere.

February 3, Gilli Trewangan

Another picturesque island – white beaches, unpolluted sea. Too paranoid about sharks to swim. Very difficult to express all my feelings and emotions because there are so many. Not missing England's luxuries but do miss family. Everybody so friendly.

Feb 8, Malang, Java

I guess stewed flies and noodles, pneumatic drills in your wall at midnight, drivers with a death-wish and dodgy tummy are what travelling is about. I've found a new meaning for 'heaven' – England.

March 1, Melaka, Malaysia

Arrived 11pm and promptly whisked away to an Indian (arranged) Wedding. Couple not too impressed with each other. Were given curry and rice on banana leaves to eat in true Indian style – with our fingers – definitely enhanced the flavour. Sophie went to the clinic with 250 mosquito bites – she looks as if she's got measles.

March 4, Melaka

Visited jungle to see Orang-Asli tribe people. Was expecting extremely primitive way of life. Found bamboo huts with TV and stereos and people tucking into pre-packed instant food. Saw beautiful waterfall alive with turtles.

March 11, Melaka

Up 7.30a.m. It's fiesta day. Whole hostel (travellers like us) dressed in traditional Hindu dress – girls in Saris, men in white shirts and sashes. Worried the locals would be offended but they were actually pleased. What a kaleidoscope of colour!

March 14, Cameron Highlands

Sat soul searching with Sid, another nomad from Europe, till dawn. Very 'ecologically sound'. You meet the oddest people on a trip like this.

April 26, Delhi, India

India at last. Very westernised, very hot, 32 centigrade at 1a.m. Everybody speaks English. Broke first rule in traveller's handbook, allowed chatty Indian (male) who picked us up in the Wimpy, (yes they have them here too) to take us to his antique/silks shop. Luckily he was OK. He gave us lunch and we gave him flowers. How touching! Saw the Taj Mahal in Agra – what can you say? Mind blowing!

May 9, Calcutta, India
Invited to visit Mother Theresa's missions – incredible atmosphere – but such a little island of help in a sea of so much misery – it seems hopeless.

June 5, Delhi
Set off for trek up the Himalayas. By 4.30p.m. was absolutely exhausted. Sophie had stomach pains so turned back. Should have gone with her. Couldn't make scheduled destination – slept in lodge very basic, primitive food cooked on mud stoves.

June 7, Kyagin Gompa
3840 m high – Indescribable. Amazing glaciers, snowy peaks. Worth all the effort, aches, pain and months of travel.

June 30th . . . . .
Our last night. Brain in state of numbness. How will I adapt again to Western culture? There have been many highs, and certainly some lows but without doubt an incredible experience.

Reason 7: Altruism – voluntary work

Voluntary work abroad in Third World countries is not so easy to find as it once was, especially if you have no recognized skill, and many organizations seek people over 21. Some projects will pay maintenance costs, and sometimes give pocket money, but it is not unusual for volunteers to be asked to pay their own fares.

Conservation work is much easier to find, both in the UK and abroad. Once again, most of it is completely voluntary and unpaid. You might even be asked to contribute to food and accommodation. You could become involved in projects for the National Trust, the Royal Society for the Protection of Birds, on the restoration of cathedrals, working with the handicapped and underprivileged children, painting, decorating – it's amazing what some students turn their hands to.

While the financial returns on both voluntary and conservation work are likely to be zero, in terms of your CV it could be of considerable value. Employers are impressed by altruistic and enterprising qualities needed for voluntary work.

Who to contact

● National Trust – Acorn Projects run more than 350 Conservation Working Holidays a year throughout England, Wales and Northern Ireland for as little as £36 for a week's full board and lodging (from

£15 for a weekend). A chance to stay in some of the most beautiful corners of the country. Full details from Acorn Project, PO Box Melksham, SN12 8SU, enclosing large SAE and 2 second class stamps.

● BTCV (British Trust for Conservation Volunteers) run some 600 conservation holidays and a number of shorter, weekend breaks from about £30 p.w. upwards. Pond maintenance, tree-planting, step-building, hedge-laying, scrub clearance, drystone walling – the options are endless. Contact BTCV at 36 St Mary's Street, Wallingford, Oxfordshire OX10 0EU. Tel: 0491 839766.

What to read

● *The International Directory of Voluntary Work* – gives details of over 500 organizations which recruit all types of volunteers for projects in all parts of the world. It's the A–Z of voluntary work: from Vacation Work (address above).

● *The Directory of Work & Study in Developing Countries* – an authoritative guide to employment, voluntary work and academic opportunities in the Third World. Ideal for those who want to experience life there as more than a tourist. Over 400 organizations in over 100 countries are listed. Short- and long-stay openings in engineering, disaster relief, agriculture, business, archaeology, construction, community work, medicine: from Vacation Work (address above).

When should I apply for holiday work?

As soon as possible. There are literally thousands of students looking for work. Most of the directories offering vacation work are printed in January, but there's nothing to stop you making a move before then.

CAN'T AFFORD THE BOOKS SUGGESTED? LOOK IN YOUR LIBRARY

Nearly all the books mentioned here should be found in the reference section of your local public library, and if they are not, your library might well order them for you. A group of you might think it worth while to buy some of the publications mentioned.

Is it a good idea to work?

If you are struggling to keep your head above water with your academic study then the advice has to be no, certainly during term time.

If you feel that by taking a year off you might not be able to get back into the rhythm of studying again, again the answer has to be no.

If lack of funds means you can't really afford to make full use of all the extracurricular opportunities your university or college offers, then the answer has to be yes.

If you are skint, with an overdraft which is crippling you on interest, then you probably have no option.

If you've had your fill of academic study and need a break, then work would be a good idea.

These are the extremes. If you don't fall fully into any of these categories – and most students don't – then the best solution is probably to 'mix and match'. In other words, work to secure your financial situation and provide yourself with new experiences and the financial resources to enjoy even more. Six weeks humping boxes in a factory could in itself give you a valuable insight into life at shop-floor level, while tuning you up both physically and financially to spend a month exploring the Sudan.

MAKING YOUR WORK EXPERIENCE WORK FOR YOU

Four years ago employers were fighting for graduates. Now, most companies are cutting back on their graduate intake. Some have opted out of the milkround*. Attendance at recruitment fairs is down. A few have stopped recruiting altogether.

As a result, employers are being swamped by applications. Many good, newly qualified students who in normal times could have expected to have several job offers to choose from are finding it difficult to get interviews, let alone a job offer. While six applications to different employers used to be ample to get an acceptance, we heard of one graduate who had written to 135 different companies without success.

* Milkround: the traditional graduate-hunting season for companies which give presentations at universities and polytechnics in the hope of winning interest and applications from students.

Don't get too depressed. The market is very volatile. By the time this year's A-level students graduate – the pendulum may well have swung, so that it's the employers who will have to do the leg and pen work. Things are beginning to look more hopeful.

But whatever the state of the employment market, the big career sort-out is very competitive. In normal times major organizations such as Barclays Bank might expect to receive around 3000 applications and usually take on 200 graduates. In these extraordinary times, applications have more than doubled. Obviously companies can interview only a small proportion of prospective applicants. So – how do they sort out the best? What are their criteria? And what do you need to have on your CV in addition to a good degree, to make you stand out from the crowd and turn an application into an interview? We asked some major employers:

'At Barclays we look first at the characteristics we need for a job, such as initiative, leadership, judgement. Then we look for evidence of these. Take initiative, for example – perhaps the candidate has travelled abroad, set up a society within college – even better, set up a business of their own to fill the vacation-job gap. Whatever you do, we want to know about it. Don't leave us guessing, because we might just guess wrong.' (Simon Thorp, recently qualified graduate working in graduate recruitment at Barclays Bank)

'Strong achievement, both socially and through personal skills, is what we are looking for. Evidence of energy with wider interests than just study. Travel, perhaps, work experience, or something you may have done at university which is outside the minimum published schedule. I also look for the black holes in an application form. Things should run in a chronological order. What you haven't mentioned may be of no interest to us, but if it's not there, it makes one wonder.' (Peter Forbes, Graduate Recruitment Manager, ICL)

'To avoid falling at the first hurdle, your application form must pin-point your talents and accomplishments. A list in itself is not enough, what we look for is evidence. For example, trekking around Europe shows enterprise – that's a point in your favour, but it's what you learnt from the experience that interests us. Did you organize the trip? Plan the route? Deal with a crisis? Good communicators, team players, time management skills, energy and enthusiasm are the qualities we are mainly looking for' (Josie Phillips, Graduate Recruitment Manager, KPMG Peat Marwick)

'We are looking for the next generation of senior managers and technical experts, the people who will drive our business forward, so the kind of

qualities we are seeking – conceptual and analytical thought, strong personal skills, ability to influence and motivate others – can't all be demonstrated through a good academic record, important though it is. We want to know about other areas of achievement.' (Margaret Harris, Graduate Recruitment, ICI)

Fact check

84 per cent of students we canvassed said they worked because they needed the money.
73 per cent of employers we canvassed said they like the graduates they take on to have had previous work experience.

THE STUDENT TRAVEL SCENE

It's all very well to whet your appetite for travel, but how are you going to manage to get to that exotic destination? This section looks briefly at the travel scene for students.

As a student, can I get cheap travel abroad?

Yes, there are a number of travel organizations that operate special schemes for students. In fact you will find they are vying for the privilege to send you off on your travels, and often dropping the price in the process. If you decide to take the cheapest, make sure it is a reputable organization, with ABTA (Association of British Travel Agents) membership. It's better to be safe than stranded.

How do I go about getting cheap travel?

If you are already a student, your college Student Travel Office is the best place to start. There you'll find experts who will understand your particular needs and financial restraints, ready to give you advice. If you are taking a Gap year, or your college has no travel office, then there are two big names in the student travel business:

CAMPUS TRAVEL: the biggest student travel agents in the UK. They have over thirty travel shops throughout Britain, many of which are on campuses or in the YHA Adventure Shop. They also have an international network of branches in Belgium, France, Germany,

Greece, Ireland and the USA. They've been in the business for over
thirty years and know most of the wrinkles. Whether it's a working
holiday you want, an adventure holiday, to see Africa, Europe, the Far
East or the USA they will get you there.

Carmen Barrett of Campus Travel says:

'*We send students everywhere in the world – hiking across the Andes,
searching for lost Inca cities in the Peruvian jungle, canoeing in South
America, and everything in between. The student mind is very independent.
Usually they'll say, "I want a flight to [say] Kathmandu; tell me: What can
I do when I get there?" We accommodate that and understand. Most of our
work is booking cheap flights and accommodation. They do the rest. They
don't want to spend two weeks lying on the beach sunning themselves in the
Med. They are looking for a more dramatic kind of excitement.*'

Contact your local Travel Shop or Campus Travel Head Office, 52
Grosvenor Gardens, London SW1W 0AG. Tel: 071–730 3402/8111
for details of your nearest Travel Shop.

ON-CAMPUS CAMPUS TRAVEL SHOPS

Aston University, Birmingham
Dundee University
Glasgow University
Liverpool John Moores University
Liverpool University
Manchester Metropolitan University
Newcastle University
Reading University
Sheffield Hallam University

STA TRAVEL claim to be the largest organization specializing in
independent travel. They have been in business for nearly twenty years
and have a network of 120 offices spanning Asia, Australia, Europe,
New Zealand and the USA – a life-saver if you are stranded. Of these,
twenty are in the UK. They will help send you just about anywhere in
the world. Their International Help Desk means that wherever you are
you can phone in for advice – provided that is, you are within reach of a
phone. It is their policy to employ only young and well-travelled
consultants in their offices – many of them are ex-students, so you
should get sympathetic advice. The *STA Travel Guide*, their latest
travel literature, is intended as a compendium to excite the real

traveller, and with tips such as 'How to exist in the Amazon' . . . 'What to pack for the Trans-Siberian Express' . . . 'The dos and don'ts of hitch-hiking in Japan' . . . and travel anecdotes from their adventurous consultants. It does make for an interesting read.

Gillian Smith of STA Travel says:

> *'About 50 per cent of our business is done with students, and most of our staff are ex-students. The route seems to be: they use us as students, go off and travel and then come back and work for us. They then know the problems and pitfalls, have been to all corners of the globe on the cheap, and know how to advise and how to survive – that's important!'*

Contact your nearest STA Travel Office or STA Travel Head Office, Priory House, 6 Wrights Lane, London W8 6TA. Tel: 071–938 4711. For information on North America, tel: 071–937 9971; Europe, tel: 071–937 9921; Rest of the World, tel: 071–937 9962.

ON-CAMPUS OFFICES:

Birmingham University
University of London
Imperial College, London
King's College, London
London School of Economics
Loughborough University
University of Kent
Nottingham Trent University
Strathclyde University

Advice note

Never pay full fare on bus, coach, train or plane. Take advantage of rail and coach cards, bucket shops, classified ads, chartered flights, stand-by fares, advance bookings, deals offered by student travel companies.

What should I join before setting off?

There are six cards that all travel-hungry students should look into:

● **ISIC: £5.**
  ISIC stands for the International Student Identity Card. It is available to any student who is studying for more than fifteen hours a

week. The card entitles you to discounts on student charter flights, some accommodation, and in some countries admission to art galleries, museums, cinemas and other places of cultural interest. It is recognized in more than fifty countries around the world. At the time of writing it costs £5, comes with the ISIC Travel Handbook which gives you full details of the services offered, handy tips on successful travelling and places to visit in 81 countries around the world. The card is available from Council Travel, Tel: 071–437 7767, or by post from ISIC Mail Order, NUS Services, Bleaklow House, Howard Town Mill, Mill Street, Glossop SK13 8PT (add 50p p&p).

● **Under–26 card: £6.**
Currently carried by 3 million young people, this card is designed to help young people explore the world. It comes with a free 'Discount Directory' which lists all the special offers available such as low price air fares and cheap youth hosteling. As a member you will automatically receive a regular magazine keeping you up to date with exchange trips, projects, events and offers. The card also gives you access to the 24-hour Travellers Help Line which will help with any difficulties you may have. It can be used in the UK as well where cardholders can get reductions at many budget hostels, leisure and cultural attractions, and in Europe where a futher 200,000 discounts are available. Contact: National Youth Agency, 52 Grosvenor Gardens, Victoria, London SW1 WOAG. Tel: 071–823 5363. Look out for special promotions on the card itself!

● **YHA: £3 (under 18) £19 (18+)**
The Youth Hostel Association (who also provide a card) offer membership of the international YHA, which gives you access to youth hostels across 56 countries. They probably wouldn't merit even a one-star rating, but they are cheap, safe – and *there*. Membership at the time of writing is £3 under 18, and £9 over 18 for UK residents. For non-UK residents there is an International Youth Hostel Federation card, which costs slightly more – all available from The Youth Hostel Association, Trevelyan House, 8 St Stephen's Hill, St Albans, Herts AL1 2DY. Tel: 07278 55215.

● **YMCA – Interpoint Programme: £2**
Through this programme the YMCA provide cheap accommo-dation for young travellers across Europe. Membership is just £2 and well worth the small outlay. Contact YMCA Interpoint Programme, Rosie Williamson, European Interpoint Co-ordinator,

National Council for YMCA, St George's Buildings, 37–41 High Street, Belfast BT1 2AB. Tel: 0232 327757.

- **Young Person's Rail Card: £16**
  This entitles all young people aged 16–23 to a third off most rail fares in the UK. Did you know that it also covers the London all zone One-Day Travel Card and discounts off network cards too?

- **Student Coach Card: £7**
  This entitles all students aged 17 and over to a third off National Express, and Scottish Citylink fares; also some continental and Irish services – check with your local coach station or Victoria Coach Station, London. Tel: 071–730 0202.

Cards-to-carry checklist:

Young Person's Rail Card	£16
Coach Card	£7
ISIC	£5
Under-26 card	£6
YHA card	£3 (under 18)
	£9 (18+)
YMCA card	£2

Who else could I consult?

The National Tourist Office or Board. Many countries have a national tourist office or board in this country. Most are based in London. London telephone directories can usually be found in the reference section of your local library.

Council Travel is part of the Council on International Educational Exchange. It offers low-cost student/youth air fares worldwide, on-the-spot ticketing, Eurotrain and Inter-Rail cards, Youth Hostel Passes and travel insurance with exceptionally low rates, and has over 30 offices worldwide. Contact: Council Travel, 28A Poland Street, London W1V 3DB. Tel: for Europe 071–287 3337; worldwide 071–437 7767.

What to read

- *The Student Guide*, published by *Time Out* Magazine and the National Union of Students, has a useful chapter on travel and a list of people to contact.

● The *Rough Guide* series covers almost every country and provides a useful insight into an area. Published by Harrap; cost varies according to the country. Try your local library.

Inter-railing or Eurotrain: what are they? What's the difference? Which is best?

They are both discount train tickets designed to enable you to see as much of Europe as cheaply as possible.

The Inter-Rail ticket entitles you to one month's unlimited travel on the railways of Europe. It is available to UK citizens and those who have been resident here for six months. There are two tickets on offer under the scheme. The youth ticket for those under 26 costs £249, and gives unlimited travel across 27 countries. The over 26 ticket costs £269 and offers travel limited largely to countries east of Germany. For full information contact any major British Rail Station or Campus Travel.

The Eurotrain ticket is for the more organized traveller. It lasts for two months and covers a route pre-arranged by you to suit your interests, sense of adventure and more importantly, budget. You can stop off anywhere along the route and for however long you want. Cost varies depending on destination. For example: how about the Eastern Explorer covering London to Amsterdam, Berlin, Prague, through Hungary, Vienna, Zurich, Brussels and back to London for £237; or London, Amsterdam, Brussels and back home for just £85. To find out more contact your nearest Campus Travel shop.

Advice Note

Find out about any rail passes offered by individual European countries. Campus Travel should be able to help you out.

As a student, do I need insurance?

Here the advice is: yes, you generally do need insurance when travelling abroad. Some work camps and voluntary agencies arrange insurance for those taking part in projects. Check this out, and check what it covers. There are certain reciprocal arrangements for medical treatment in some EC countries. Check out the details and get Department of Social Security leaflet SA 28/30.

Travel insurance: how much will it cost? What should it cover?

For as little as £12 for six days' travel the International Student Insurance Service (ISIS) will provide insurance cover for your baggage, ticket and health. Most student travel companies will sell ISIS. Take it out when you buy your ticket. The cost will vary depending on how far you are going and how much cover you want. Don't forget to read the small print.

Price guide
6 days cover £12–£29
14 days cover £16–£36
6 months in Europe – £110
6 months worldwide – £189
6 months study abroad Europe – £88
  NB Cover for students studying is 20% less
6 months study abroad worldwide – £131.20
12 months study abroad Europe £164
12 months study abroad worldwide £263.20

For details contact Endsleigh Insurance Services Ltd, Endsleigh House, Ambrose Street, Cheltenham, Gloucestershire GL50 3NR. Tel: 0242 223300. They will then refer you to your nearest branch.

Letter home

Andrew Cray is reading Computer Science at the University of Wales, Aberystwyth. Last year he took a year out through the Aberystwyth YES scheme (see page 100) and joined Sandoz Pharma AG in Basle, Switzerland where he worked in software development and computer user support, while using the opportunity to explore Europe. On this next page he tells of his experiences in a letter to friends.

Aberystwyth
November

Dear All

Close your eyes and picture the scene: a landscape of icy Alpine peaks buttressed by steep slopes wooded heavily with pine. The deep midwinter snow lining the branches glistens and sparkles in the weak December sun; warm, heated chalets glow from the silent depths of the valley below as the pointed spire of the village churches rises above them. Open your eyes! Wouldn't you just love to be in Switzerland?

That's where I spent last year working for Sandoz, a giant pharmaceutical firm based in Basle, working with computers. Every year they employ hundreds of students like me, from all over the world, who come not only to work, but to enjoy what Switzerland has to offer – the clean environment, the ski resorts of St Moritz and Klosters, hikes through the Alpine pastures, travel and the cosmopolitan feel of a country in the very heart of Europe.

Cuckoo clocks, gold watches and the chime of cow bells! It's more than that. Switzerland may be conservative, but it is also alive with people of all nationalities and the cities bulge with optimism. The rosy picture is tainted only by a discreet scattering of hard drug addicts on the streets of Basle and Zurich; it would be wrong for me not to warn you about them, for I saw them every day.

But as a base for exploring continental Europe, Switzerland cannot easily be beaten. My year in employment meant travel to the glamour of Cannes and Monte Carlo, the Renaissance charm of romantic Italy and the Bohemian splendour of rediscovered Prague. Places I could never have afforded to visit as an impoverished student.

Best wishes

Andrew

5
OTHER SOURCES TO TAP

Trusts, charitable awards, scholarships, bursaries, competitions

In this chapter we investigate all the other legitimate sources of finance you could tap to raise extra cash, and how to set about approaching them. They include trusts, charitable awards, scholarships, bursaries, competitions.

FAST FACTS ON ALTERNATIVE SOURCES OF FINANCE

Who gives bursaries and scholarships?	Charitable trusts, universities and colleges, professional bodies and institutions
How much?	From £17 to £2,000 and everything in between
Will an award affect my grant?	No
What is the success rate?	Low

Other sources of finance: a reality or a vain hope?

You are right to be a little sceptical. If there were a prodigious number of organizations, all eager to hand out money to students, you wouldn't have seen so many student demonstrations called to highlight their financial plight. But there are a surprising number of educational charities, trust funds and foundations, professional bodies, and benevolent funds available in this country which offer financial help to students. This may take the form of a scholarship or charitable award. One directory of grant-making trusts we consulted listed over 1,500 organizations under the broad heading of Education. But before you get too excited and think you've found the route to a crock of gold, when you start sifting through the many restrictions which trusts generally have to abide by, you soon realize there are relatively few – if any – that could meet your exact needs.

What is a scholarship?

Scholarships differ from sponsorships by providing money while you study without the industrial training. They can, of course, be for a specific purpose like travel, to fund some special area of research, or possibly to study abroad. They are usually, though not always, given by institutions – this could be your university, a professional institute or a charitable trust – rather than by individual companies.

Competition is keen. Awards can be made on grounds of academic achievement or need. Whatever the criteria, they are not going to come your way without considerable effort and often disappointment, so be prepared. Nobody gives money away easily.

What is a charitable award?

The difference between a scholarship and a charitable award is very indistinct, and you could say there is no difference at all, as charitable awards can often be scholarships. Charitable awards are always paid out by a charitable organization which must abide by the terms and conditions of the original endowment. So however good and reason-able your case may be, if the money has to be paid out to a student from Gloucester studying Chemistry, it is no good being an Arts student from Leeds. To claim an award, both you and your financial predicament must fit the charity's help profile.

What kind of awards are available?

Often the payments are small – to buy books, or equipment – but they can be quite substantial and cover fees or maintenance. So it could be from a few hundred pounds to a few thousand. They can be one-off payments, or given each year for the duration of your course.

FINDING OUT ABOUT TRUSTS AND SCHOLARSHIPS

Can my school help me?

Yes, most schools will have a list of local charities which offer help to students. The fact that you have been to the school could be a condition of receiving a grant. Also try your primary school. It is a good idea to find out if such scholarships and bursaries are available before you send off your UCAS application, as these sometimes stipulate a certain higher education establishment.

Can my local authority help?

They should have details of any local charities which offer help to students in higher education.

Try also

- The Welsh Office – they offer bursaries to Welsh-born students attending Welsh universities.

- The Carnegie Trust for the Universities of Scotland, which provides financial assistance to students of Scottish birth or extraction, or with at least two years' secondary education in Scotland, wanting to attend Scottish universities. They also offer vacation scholarships to enable undergraduates to undertake a research project during the long vacation. Contact Carnegie Trust for the Universities of Scotland, 22 Hanover Street, Edinburgh, Scotland EH2 2EN.

- The Scottish Education Department maintains a Register of Educational Endowments on Scottish trusts, many of which are local and open only to Scottish-born students wanting to attend Scottish universities. The Educational Department will search the Register on behalf of any student who submits an enquiry form. Forms are available from The Scottish Office Education Department, Students' Award Branch, Gyleview House, 3 Redheughs Rigg, Edinburgh EH12 9HH.

Check out your parents' employers!

Or at least get them to. A surprising number of companies and large employers have special trusts set up to help with the education of their employees' or past employees' children. Typical examples:

● The Miners' Welfare National Education Fund for dependants of those working in the coal-mining industry;

● The National Police Fund, which helps the children of people who are serving in or have served in the police force;

● The Royal Medical Benevolent Fund, which helps the children of medical graduates, and the Dain Fund Charities Committee (contact the BMA), which helps the children of registered members of the medical profession;

● The Royal Pinner School Foundation, which helps the children of sales representatives.

Do universities and colleges give scholarships?

Some higher education institutions are endowed by generous benefactors and can award scholarships and bursaries to selected students who meet the required criteria. Usually an institution will have a very mixed bag of awards which bears very little relation to its academic strengths and interests. Most establishments don't give many awards, and competition is generally keen. Drop in the ocean or not, it is certainly worth a try. Many of the scholarships have a subject or location condition attached, which does considerably limit those eligible to apply.

How much would a college scholarship be worth?

Awards vary in amounts tremendously: some are given annually for the full three to four years of a course, while others are a one-off payment. The highest awards seem to be around £2,000 and the lowest we discovered was at Aberystwyth, for just £17.50.

How would I go about getting a college scholarship?

Scholarship distribution methods differ with each institution and, of course, the terms of the foundation. Aberystwyth, for example, holds formal examinations during January each year. It gives 20–25 entry scholarships worth around £600 a year. Entries need to be in by mid-December. Aberdeen University also holds a competitive examination towards the end of March. Being an old university, they are well endowed, and offer some sixty bursaries a year worth around £30,000 on the basis of this examination. The bursaries range from £100 to £600 p.a. paid throughout the course of study. Aberdeen also offer a fair range of endowed prizes of various kinds. There is no charge for entering the examination, and candidates can sit it at Aberdeen University – accommodation provided free – or in Inverness, Stornoway, Lerwick, Kirkwall or Glasgow. In exceptional cases a candidate can take the examination at their own school.

First look in the college prospectus – it should either list the awards given, or give you an address to write to for details. This should be done early in the autumn term of your final school year and before or about the time you are filling in your UCAS form. Obviously at this stage you do not know which university you are likely to go to, but – as with Aberystwyth – the exams can be held early in the academic year, before you have made your final decision.

What about the professional institutions? Do they give scholarships?

Some do, some don't. The engineering institutions are among the most generous. Awards are made to students studying IEE-accredited degree courses:

- Institution of Electrical Engineers (IEE), Savoy Place, London WC2R 0BL. Tel: 071–240 1871: give 12 scholarships of £500 p.a. for the duration of the degree course. Plus 30 Engineering Scholarships of £750 for women.

- Institution of Civil Engineers, Queen's Jubilee Scholarship Trust, 1–7 Great George Street, London SW1P 3AA. Tel: 071–222 7722: award valued at £1,000 p.a. for the duration of the degree course, usually 30 given.

- British Paper and Board Industry Federation, Papermakers House, Rivenhall Road, Westlea, Swindon SN5 7BE: Rackley Scholarship £1,000 p.a. for the duration of the course, usually 3 given.

- Institution of Mechanical Engineers, Northgate Avenue, Bury St

Edmunds, Suffolk IP32 6BN: Whitworth Scholarships – 10 awarded, currently valued at £1,300 p.a. Given to engineers taking a degree who left full-time education at an early age, generally 16.

● Company of Chartered Surveyors, 16 St Mary-at-Hill, London EC3R 8EE: offer assistance to students in their final year of a first degree course in surveying.

● Institute of Marine Engineers, The Memorial Building, 76 Mark Lane, London EC3R 7JN: offer bursaries to selected students of up to £700 p.a., plus scholarships valued at £800 p.a. to students studying at Robert Gordon University, Aberdeen; Heriot-Watt University, Edinburgh; Liverpool John Moores University; University of Newcastle upon Tyne; and the University of Surrey.

● The Mineral Industries Educational Trust, 6 St James's Square, London SW1Y 4LD. Tel: 071-753 21187. Awards are given to students studying honours degrees in mining, quarrying, mineral processing, extractive metallurgy, and applied geology. Some MSc courses are also sponsored. Bursaries: £1,250 p.a., with exceptional students gaining scholarships of £1,750 p.a.

What charities and trusts help students, and how would I get in touch with them?

In the next few pages we list some of the charitable organizations where you could apply for financial help. This is by no means an exhaustive list, but it will give you a head start. Addresses and more details can be found in the directories listed opposite, which should be available in your local library.

Books to read
● *The Grants Register*, published by Macmillan
● *Directory of Grant-Making Trusts*, published by the Charities Aid Foundation
● *The Educational Grants Directory* published by the Directory of Social Change
● *Charities Digest*, published by the Family Welfare Association
● *Money to Study*, published by the Family Welfare Association

Advice note

Before making an application to a charity, it is important to be clear in your own mind exactly what kind of student they are likely to help, and what kind of financial assistance you are after, otherwise you could be wasting both your own time and theirs.

TRUSTS AND CHARITIES WHICH SPECIFICALLY HELP DISABLED STUDENTS

Arthritis Care
British Association of Health Services in Higher Education
Drapers' Charitable Fund
The Peter Greenwood Memorial Trust for the Deaf or Hearing Impaired
Institution of Electrical Engineers – The Lord Hirst Fund
Mary MacArthur Educational Trust
The Hilda Martindale Educational Trust
Royal National Institute for the Blind
Royal National Institute for the Deaf
Snowdon Award Scheme

TRUSTS AND CHARITIES WHICH HELP THOSE STUDYING SPECIFIC SUBJECTS

ACCOUNTANCY:
   Association of Certified Accountants: Certified Accountant's Jubilee Scholarships
AERONAUTICS:
   Royal Aeronautical Society
AGRICULTURE:
   The William Scott Abbott Trust
   Douglas Bomford Trust
   Royal Bath & West Southern Counties Society Travelling Scholarships
ARCHITECTURE:
   Architects' Registration Council of the United Kingdom
CHEMISTRY:
   Royal Society of Chemistry Marriott Bequest Scheme

COMMERCE/COMPUTER/BUSINESS STUDIES:
  Koettgen Memorial Fund
DENTISTRY:
  General Dental Council Charitable Trust
LAW:
  Bar Council Students' Loan Fund and The Bar Council's Trust
  Funds Committee
  Chambers Pupillage Awards
  The Council of Legal Education Inns of Court Studentships
  Law Society Bursary and Loan Schemes
  Solicitors Benevolent Association
MEDICINE:
  Lord Ashdown Charitable Trust
  BMA Medical Education Trust
MUSIC:
  Benslow Musical Instrument Loan Scheme
  Gerald Finzi Charitable Trust
  Martin Musical Scholarship Fund
  Royal Society of Musicians of Great Britain
MUSIC, DRAMA, VISUAL ARTS:
  Berkwickshire Educational Trust
  Bird's Charity – Royal Academy of Arts
PHARMACISTS:
  The Royal Pharmaceutical Society's Benevolent Fund
SCIENCE AND ENGINEERING:
  The Caroline Haslett Memorial Trust (mainly to women)
  Students' Aid Fund – Institution of Mechanical Engineers
  Worshipful Company of Scientific Instrument Makers
  Worshipful Company of Shipwrights (maritime subjects)

What sort of help do trusts give?

Help with fees, maintenance, books, equipment, travel either to and from your college or abroad, special sports activities, childminding, special projects. They all vary in what they will offer, and to whom.

Is there anybody who could advise me on applying to charitable trusts?

EGAS, which stands for the Education Grants Advisory Service and is part of the Family Welfare Association, will advise students on organizations to contact. They have a comprehensive database of charities and trusts. If you write to them, setting out briefly your financial predicament and needs, they will dip into their extensive files and see who are the most likely bodies to help you. With their list of names and addresses comes a helpful leaflet on how to approach charities. Write to EGAS, c/o The Family Welfare Association, 501–505 Kingsland Road, Dalston, London E8 4AU. If you want help on how to write to EGAS phone them on 071–254 6251 and ask to be connected to their recorded message service.

What are my chances? How likely am I to hit the jackpot?

Slim, though the odds are certainly better than the likelihood of winning the pools. Competition is keen, and with the reduction in student grants, it's going to get keener. In 1989 the Education Grants Advisory Service received just 2,856 written applications from students; by 1990 that had risen to 4000. Last year they received over 10,000 written applications and this year they expect a deluge. *'Trusts at the moment are overwhelmed with applications, but occasionally students do hit the jackpot,'* says Belinda Savile, Student Adviser at EGAS. *'It's important that students give us precise information about their circumstances so we can marry suitable candidates to suitable trusts. Trusts usually have specific criteria on which they can give funds and most are only a few hundred pounds. Postgraduates do come to us asking for say £2,000 for fees and another £4,000 for living expenses. That's a lot to find, you have to go to a lot of trusts. The fact is, the less you ask for the more likely you are to be helped.'*

EGAS does in fact offer a number of small grants itself to students for particular needs. These are usually small – up to £200 and for something specific like a computer or equipment for a hairdressing course. Childminding is one of the major areas where students ask for help which, says Joan Dixon who administers grant applications, is very difficult to deal with because it is so expensive and is generally for such a long time. EGAS handle about 40 grants a month and most are given to help students in their final year. Typical examples:

● for books or equipment
● a parent is suddenly made redundant and can't continue to finance fees;
● a student, who has been paying their way through part-time work, feels they need to give it up for that final two month push.

Last word from Assistant Ann Thomas: '*People contact us as their last hope. They are expecting miracles which of course we can only rarely work.*'

When should I contact a trust?

Most trusts have an application deadline. This is usually given along with the information in the trust and grants directories. Check out each entry carefully; they are all different. Trusts are not the answer for a fast financial fix. Like all bodies, they tend to move exceedingly slowly. Your case would have to be scrutinized along with many others, so it could be months before you get an answer.

Could I get through higher education funded only by a charitable trust?

It could be done, but don't depend on it. Many charities won't consider you until you have tried all the usual channels available to students, and they do tend to give help towards the end of a course, rather than the beginning.

If I get help from a charity, will it affect my grant?

No. Charitable awards and scholarships, like sponsorships, will not affect your grant, and are unlikely to bring your finances into the tax bracket.

Can I apply to more than one charity?

Yes, but blanket saturation is not advisable. Limit your applications to organizations which are really likely to give you funds.

How do I go about applying to a charity?

There are no set rules. What one charitable trust wants, another doesn't. Here is a general procedure to follow:

1 Put together a list of suitable charities *either* by consulting the list in this book, EGAS, or the directories in the library.
2 Find out exactly what each charity is offering by consulting the directories listed earlier in this chapter. Check if there is any date by which your entry must be in.

3 Write a brief note to the charities you consider most suitable, explaining your need and asking for any details about the charity, and if they have an application form.
4 Photocopy any application form you are sent before starting to fill it in so that you can have a dummy run. A form full of crossings-out does not create the best impression.
5 Fill in the application form. Make sure your answers are clear and truthful. You may be questioned on it later. There will probably be a section asking you to give details of why you are in need of financial assistance. Try to be concise without missing out any relevant facts. Bear the trust's criteria in mind.
6 Photocopy the completed form before you send it back. You need to know exactly what you have said, and the details may be useful for subsequent forms.
7 Wait patiently. These things can take many weeks to process.

Do students actually get help?

'As an Engineering student I needed a computer, but couldn't afford one. Were there are charities that could help? I searched around, and discovered the Earl's Colne Educational Trust, which assisted students living within ten miles of Earl's Colne in Essex. I lived in Halstead, just within the limits – it was worth a try. I wrote to them explaining my needs; they sent me a form; I filled it in; I waited; I went for an interview. The result: £500 – easy money. It cost just two sides of A4!' (Jonathan Wilson, 20, studying Electronic Engineering at Loughborough University)

COMPETITIONS – ARE THEY A WORTHWHILE OPTION?

Competitions are not a very reliable or constant source of finance, but again you may be lucky. Occasionally companies or newspapers will run competitions. The prize can be money, books, travel, or the chance to work abroad for that company. They are usually one-off opportunities.

If it's a competition set especially for students, it very often involves writing an essay. Students, being the overworked – or is it lazy! – people they are, tend to give them a miss, so the number of entries can be poor. All the more reason to give it a try.

Several years ago the Chartered Accountancy firm KPMG Peat Marwick ran such a competition, and seven lucky undergraduates won the chance to work for six weeks for the firm in such faraway places as São Paulo, Toronto, Cologne, Melbourne, Sydney, Harare and Tai Pei. They were given an open air-fare ticket which gave them a chance to travel, earned six weeks' salary and invaluable work experience. Not bad for a few hours' work on a 1500-word essay.

The Independent ran a travel writing competition in conjunction with Fodor's the publishers. The first prize was a round-the-world air ticket worth £1,000, plus £500 spending money, all for a 1,000 word article.

The drawback with competitions is that the winner takes all and the many also-rans get nothing. Still, it's worth keeping your eyes skinned.

Where to look

- On your college noticeboard
- In the careers office
- National newspapers
- Student newspapers.

6
TIGHTEN YOUR BELTS

Funding for Postgraduates

Postgraduates are proliferating. In the last ten years the number of students on postgraduate courses has almost doubled. How are they managing to pay for their studies? Has funding kept pace with the demand? In this chapter we look at the main sources of finance for postgraduates.

How many postgraduates are there?

According to a survey commissioned by the Department for Education the number of UK (home) students on full-time postgraduate courses was 65,900 in 1991–92. Today the figure is undoubtedly higher.

Which are the boom areas for postgraduate study?

The biggest growth has been in university Masters courses especially in medicine-related degrees, business MBAs and computing based courses. Social sciences and the humanities are also increasing in popularity. Lowest rise is in engineering and technology.

Is it worth taking a postgraduate qualification?

Yes, if it's a subject you are particularly interested in or if it is a vocational course, and certainly if you are seeking a post in academia or a research-based organisation. But there is no real evidence to suggest that in general further qualifications will help you secure a job.

How much will it cost?

Tuition Fees:

UK Residents and EC Nationals
Likely fee 1993/4   £2,260 p.a.
(Certain courses may be higher: Legal Practice Course £4,600 p.a.;
MBA £10K.)

Students from abroad   Arts – £5,550
Recommended minimum 1993/4   Science – £7,360
                                                                     Clinical – £13,550

Maintenance:

The results of our research given in Chapter 1 will give you some idea. However, standards for Postgraduates tend to be higher. Leeds University Union budget advice book to students suggests a single student would need a minimum of £6,511 (male) £6,877 (female) if living in university self-catering accommodation and £6,550 (male) and £6,916 (female) in the private rented sector. In London we would suggest a figure of £7,500–£10,000.

Will I get funding?

Don't bank on it. Competition for funding for postgraduates is phenomenal. There is no all-embracing funding system as for first degrees and students generally have to search around to get help. It is much easier to get a place on a course than it is to get the money to pay for it. Many postgraduates have to finance themselves with loans etc, which is probably why part-time study for postgraduates is increasing in popularity. If you are offered funding make sure it covers both tuition fees and maintenance.

When should I start considering taking a postgraduate course?

At least a year before you graduate.

What are the possible sources for funding?

1 **Government Funding from Research Councils and the British Academy** – These are by far the largest sources of funding in the UK. Last year, they made some 7,730 awards. Each

'awarding body' funds different courses and there is no overlap, so it is important to identify the appropriate body for your needs (see this chapter).

2 **Department For Education and Home Office** – They largely fund vocational or professional courses (see this chapter).

3 **ERASMUS** – Programme developed by the European Commission to provide funds for the mobility of students and staff in universities throughout the 12 EC member states and the countries of the European Free Trade Association (EFTA). See page 42 for full details and information on LINGUA, COMMETT and TEMPUS.

4 **Employers** – Employers will occasionally sponsor employees through courses, especially MBAs.

5 **Companies** – May sponsor students on a research project. This could be as the result of a work experience association during a first degree, or in cooperation with one of the research councils (see CASE this chapter).

6 **Trusts & Charities** – More likely to award small amounts of money rather than full financial support, but certainly worth considering. (See chapter 5 Other Sources to Tap.) Your Local Authority Awards Officer would have details of any local charities. Otherwise contact EGAS (see page 128 for details) or look in the published charities and grant-making trusts directories and registers. Apply early, processing can be inordinately slow.

7 **Local Authorities** – Except in the case of teacher training, Local Authorities are not required by law to fund postgraduates. Funding is discretionary, is given mainly for vocational courses which lead to certificates or diplomas, is means tested and criteria differ between authorities. Likely subjects are accountancy, journalism, law, music, secretarial work, youth work, computing. If you are tapping your local authority it is essential to apply early as their funds are limited, and you'll need to put up a good case for yourself. But, because there are no set rules for funding, it is always worth a try. Applications should be made by March/April.

8 **Universities Own Postgraduate Studentship Awards** – Many insitutions have a small number of studentships available for specific courses. Aberystwyth for example gives about 10 awards in

total which could be for one or three years for research degrees. Awards cover fees and maintenance. Closing date for applications May 1st (Arts and Humanities), June 1st (Sciences). Check your university of choice for details.

9 **University Departments** – They may have nothing, and probably won't advertise. But, if they particularly want you, or there's something they are interested in doing they may have sources they can tap. You could find they stipulate that you have to take on some tutorial work or assist the department.

   Tip from Gina Preston of Aberystwyth's Postgraduate Admissions Officer: *'I say to graduates its always worth a try, all it needs is the right phone call just at the right time'.*

10 **Research Assistantships:** – These are salaried posts in academic departments which provide the opportunity to study for a higher degree. Salaries vary and opportunities can become available throughout the year. Watch the relevant press for adverts – Guardian, Times, New Scientist, Nature etc.

11 **Loans from Banks:** – See later in this chapter.

Can I get a student loan?

Only if you are taking a Postgraduate Certificate in Education (PGCE). *Plus point*: even though it's generally only a one year course, you will be classed as a first rather than a final year student so can take out the maximum loan offered. Otherwise NO. Try a bank loan (see page 154).

Who exactly are the award-making bodies?

These are the main sources of government funding for postgraduates. There are around ten major award-making bodies in the UK. Each one operates independently and the awards they offer are all slightly different, as are their regulations. The information given here should, therefore, be seen as a general guide to what you could expect to get. All the award-making bodies issue information about their own awards which can be gained by writing or phoning them individually (addresses are given later in this chapter). There has been a reorganization of the Research Councils – new names have arrived on the scene and old ones have disappeared – which makes the situation rather confusing, so make sure any information you get is up-to-date.

What kind of government award could I get?

Basically there are four kinds of awards for postgraduate students:

- A Research Studentship, which is generally a three year award leading to a doctorate (PhD or DPhil).
- A Collaborative Research Studentship, when the research project is part-funded by an outside industrial organization and may well give the student some experience outside the academic environment. The collaborating company generally gives the student extra cash on top of the studentship award. The awarding body may also give an additional £250 on top of the basic studentship. This is certainly the situation with CASE (Co-operative Awards in Science and Engineering) students.
- Advanced Course Studentships. These are given for taught courses which must be of at least six months duration, but are generally for one year, often leading to a Master's (MSc, MA) or other qualification.
- Bursaries, which are allocated by the Department For Education to selected institutions for selected postgraduate courses – largely professional or vocational. The institution then nominates the candidate for the award.

Not all awarding bodies give all types of award. And some give additional awards and fellowships.

Is the award means tested?

It depends on the body. Some awards are means tested on parents' or spouse's income, some on spouse's income alone and some not at all.

What could an award cover?

- payment of approved fees to the institution
- maintenance allowance
- dependants' and other allowances
- assistance with additional travel and subsistence expenses for something like fieldwork

Do I have to get a 2.1 to take a postgraduate course?

Each course will set its own requirements. If you are thinking of specializing in your degree subject, a 1st or 2.1 is probably what you will need. For a vocational course, you'll need to show real commitment and interest in the subject. If, however, you are seeking funding from a government funding council then, they will generally demand:

- a first or upper-second class honours degree or a lower-second with a further qualification such as an MA for a Research Studentship;
- at least a lower-second honours degree for a taught/one year course. (This does not apply to Social or Probationary work courses.)

Which is easiest to get – funding for a one-year course or a three-year PhD?

A change in thinking by the Government outlined in a recent White Paper on science suggests that from now on it will be easier to gain funding for a one-year taught course than for a PhD. This is because in future PhD students will normally be expected to have taken a formal Masters training programme to be considered for a PhD studentship.

How do I go about getting funding?

Start with your university careers office. Most are very on the ball when it comes to tapping the meagre resources available to postgraduates. They may even publish a special leaflet on sources of funding for postgraduate study. Many of the publications listed at the end of this chapter which we suggest you consult should also be in the university careers library. Talk, also, to the tutors in your department, especially if you are wanting to undertake a research degree, as they will know what projects are likely to gain funding. Consult university prospectuses.

When should I approach the award-making bodies?

If you want general information on their award scheme – any time. It is important to read thoroughly the individual information produced by the different award-making bodies as their closing dates, methods of application and what they offer will vary. In most cases application for awards is done through the institution you hope to join. Check information for procedure.

How do I apply for funding?

In the case of most research councils (BBSRC, EPSRC, MRC, NERC, PPARC), funding to students is funnelled through university departments and courses. They select the students for their courses/ projects and submit their names to the awarding body. Application forms are obtained from the department for your intended studies and must be returned to them well in advance of July 31st when the department will submit it to the appropriate awarding council.

In the case of the British Academy and Economic and Social Research Council (ESRC), awards are allocated by competition. Having secured an offer of a place on a course, students apply for an award through their referees. Applications must be with the appropriate awarding body by May 1st, so again make sure your application is with your course 'organisers' long before then.

Will it make a difference where I choose to study?

Yes. Not all courses or departments attract funding. It is important to find out the situation when you apply. And just because a course is eligible for studentships, and you have a place on that course, it still doesn't mean you will necessarily get one. It is very competitive. And remember, if you don't get funding it could mean not only paying your own maintenance but also course fees. Then a university close to your own home might be the answer, or studying part-time (day release, evening courses or distance-learning).

When and how can I find out what projects have funding?

From April onwards your university should have a list of university departments that have been given funding by the awarding bodies. Under the scheme, universities are committed to attracting the very best students for the awards, so must advertise for candidates outside as well as inside their own university. Typical media: *New Scientist, Nature, The Guardian*, university magazines depending on the topic. If you want a list of which courses and projects throughout the country have received funding contact the appropriate awarding body after April 1st.

Can I approach more than one awarding body for funding?

No. There is no overlap between the awarding research councils; they each have their designated topics they fund. So, it is important to identify which body to apply to as you can only apply to one. In the case of the British Academy and the Department For Education there does appear to be some overlap. However, a course which attracts bursaries from the DFE will not generally gain funding from other state sources.

THE AWARD-MAKING BODIES

Figures quoted are for 1993–4. They are all per annum.

Subjects given for each body have been selected to give a broad view of topics covered and are by no means exhaustive. Candidates should check with the appropriate organization.

BIOTECHNOLOGY AND BIOLOGICAL SCIENCES RESEARCH COUNCIL (BBSRC) – part of the Science and Engineering Research Council.
(Formerly Agricultural and Food Research Council – AFRC)

Subject areas:	Agriculture and food science, animal and plant breeding, animal and plant pathology, biochemistry, crop protection, human nutrition, veterinary science, plant sciences, animal sciences and psychology, genetics, microbiology, development biology, popular biology and evolution, simple nervous systems IRC (Sussex), invertebrate neuroscience. Also microbial physiology, protein engineering, animal cell technology, host visitors/cell engineering, carbohydrate chemistry.
Type of award:	Research Studentship Advanced Course Studentship · Veterinary Research Fellowship
Amount:	Study in London £7,950 Elsewhere £6,200
Address:	Biotechnology and Biological Sciences Research Council Polaris House North Star Avenue Swindon SN2 1UH Tel: 0793 413200

ECONOMIC AND SOCIAL RESEARCH COUNCIL (ESRC)

Subject Area:	Accountancy, area studies, computing applied to the social sciences, criminology, economic and social history, economic and social statistics (including demography), economics, education, ethnology related to social anthropology, human geography, international relations, linguistics, management and industrial relations, marketing, planning, political sciences, psychology, social anthropology, sociology, socio-legal studies, social administration, town and country planning.
Type of Award:	Research Studentship Advanced Course Studentship
Amount:	Studying in London £6,115 p.a. Elsewhere £4,720 p.a.
Address:	Economic and Social Research Council Postgraduate Training Division Polaris House North Star Avenue Swindon SN2 1UJ Tel: 0793 413096

MEDICAL RESEARCH COUNCIL (MRC)

Subject Area:	Medicine (including tropical), areas of biology including molecules and cells, inheritance, reproduction and child health, infections and immunity (including HIV and AIDS), cancer, imaging, neurobiology, cognitive science, clinical neurosciences and mental health, health services research, clinical psychology.
Type of Award:	Research Studentship Collaborative Research Studentship Advance Course Studentship

Amount:

	1st yr	2nd yr	3rd yr
Study in London:	£8,165	£8,565	£8,975
Elsewhere	£6,145	£6,505	£6,870

NB Collaborative Studentship – additional money may be awarded to students by collaborative partner.

Address:	Medical Research Council 20 Park Crescent London W1N 4AL Tel: 071-636 5422

NATURAL ENVIRONMENT RESEARCH COUNCIL (NERC)

Subject area:	Geology, geochemistry, geophysics, physical oceanography, marine ecology, hydrology, freshwater ecology, terrestrial ecology, soil sciences, earth observation and associated science, atmospheric chemistry, science based archaeology.
Type of Award:	Research Studentship Co-operative Award in Science and Engineering (CASE) Advance Course Studentship
Amount:	Study in London £6,310 Elsewhere £4,950 NB CASE Award – additional £250 given by council, plus a minimum of £1,000 by collaborator.
Address:	Natural Environment Research Council Polaris House North Star Avenue Swindon SN2 1UH Tel: 0973 411500

ENGINEERING AND PHYSICAL SCIENCES RESEARCH COUNCIL (EPSRC)
(formerly part of the Science and Engineering Research Council SERC)

Subject Area:	Chemistry, mathematics, physics (other than that assigned to PPARC, but including nuclear structure physics), information technology, manufacturing technology, materials science and engineering.
Type of award:	Research Studentship Co-operative Awards in Science and Engineering (CASE) Advanced Course Studentship
Amount:	Studying in London £6,115 Elsewhere £4,720 (NB CASE awards – additional £250 given by Council plus minimum of £1,800 by collaborator)
Address:	Engineering and Physical Sciences Research Council Polaris House North Star Avenue Swindon SN2 1UH Tel: 0793 411000

PARTICLE PHYSICS AND ASTRONOMY RESEARCH COUNCIL (PPARC)
(formerly part of the Science and Engineering Research Council SERC)

Subject Area:	Particle physics, astronomy and astro-physics, solar system science.
Type of award:	Research Studentship Co-operative Award in Science and Engineering (CASE) Advanced Course Studentship
Amount:	Studying in London £6,115 Elsewhere £4,720 NB CASE Award – additional £250 given by Council plus minimum of £1,800 by collaborator).
Address:	Particle Physics and Astronomy Research Council Polaris House North Star Avenue Swindon SN2 1UH Tel: 0793 411000

THE BRITISH ACADEMY

Subject area:	Archaeology, art history, architecture, classics, English, history, law, linguistics, modern languages, music, philosophy, theology.
Type of award:	Doctoral Research Studentship Advance Course Studentship 1 or 2 years
Amount:	Study in London £6,115 Elsewhere £4,720
Address:	The British Academy Postgraduate Studentship Office Block 1, Spur 15, Government Buildings Honeypot Lane Stanmore Middlesex HA7 1AZ Tel: 081-951 5188

CENTRAL COUNCIL FOR EDUCATION AND TRAINING IN SOCIAL WORK (CCETSW)

Subject area: Social Work
Type of award: Bursary for Diploma in Social Work
Amount: Studying in London   £3,098
                       Elsewhere   £2,428
                       Living in parents' home   £1,818
                       NB award is means tested on parents'/spouses'
                       income.
Address: Central Council for Education and Training in Social
                       Work
                       Information Service
                       Derbyshire House
                       St Chad's Street
                       London WC1H 8AD
                       Tel: 071-278 2455

MINISTRY OF AGRICULTURE, FISHERIES AND FOOD (MAFF)

Subject area: Agriculture, horticulture and farm management
Type of award: Research Studentship
                       Co-operative Award in Science and Engineering
                       (CASE)
                       Advance Course Studentship
Amount: Studying in London   £6,900
                       Elsewhere   £5,500
                       NB CASE awards collaborator may give additional
                       funds to student but it is not mandatory.
Address: Ministry of Agriculture, Fisheries & Food
                       Room 107, Nobel House
                       17 Smith Square
                       London SW1P 3JR
                       Tel: 071-238 3000

HOME OFFICE (HO)

Subject area:	Probation Work
Type of award:	Professional Course – Diploma in Social Work
Amount:	Studying in London £3,098
	Elsewhere £2,428
	Living at home £1,818
	Plus additional £3,000 given to those with probation service experience and £1,000 for other students. Grant is means related.
Address:	Home Office
	Room 442
	Queen Anne's Gate
	London SW1H 9AT
	Tel: 071-273 2675

DEPARTMENT FOR EDUCATION (DFE)

Subject areas:	Library and information science, archive administration, art and design, drama, interpreting and translating, journalism, museum studies, pastoral studies, radio, film and TV studies, tourism.
Type of award:	Research Studentship 2 or 3 years
	Advance Course Studentship 6–12 months
	See also State Bursary, page 146.
Amount:	Studying in London £5,340
	Elsewhere £4,245
	Living with parents £3,130
Address:	Department For Education
	Mowden Hall
	Staindrop Road
	Darlington
	DL3 9BG
	Tel: 0325 392803

DEPARTMENT FOR EDUCATION (DFE) BURSARIES

Type of course:	Drama, journalism, media studies, library and information science, art and design, language interpretation, and museum studies.
Type of award:	State Bursary
Amount:	Course fees £2,260
	Studying in London £3,170
	Elsewhere £2,500
	Living with parents £1,890
	(means tested on parents'/spouses' income)
Address:	Department For Education, Bursaries
	DFE Publications Centre
	PO Box 2193
	London E15 EU
	Tel: 081-533 2000

ADDITIONAL INFORMATION ON BURSARIES

Do all postgraduate courses offer bursaries?

No, some courses don't qualify. And on courses that do, not all the students get a bursary because state bursaries are offered on a quota basis to educational institutions. Caution: courses funded at one institution may not be funded at another, even if they have the same or a similar name.

How do I know if I will get a bursary?

When you apply for a course, ask if it is eligible for bursaries. If you are offered a place then make sure which of the following the offer includes:

a) a firm nomination for a bursary
b) inclusion on a reserve list for a bursary
c) a course place with no bursary

What if I want to train as a teacher?

If you take a course leading to the Postgraduate Certificate of Education (PGCE) or specified equivalent, then you could apply for a student grant as for an undergraduate and would be eligible for a student loan at the higher, first year rates. The grant portion will be means tested on your parents'/spouses' income, and the same rules and regulations apply as for undergraduates. However, to encourage people into teaching in areas where there is a real shortage, the Department For Education offers a tax-free bursary of £1,000 p.a. in addition to any grant, to students undertaking postgraduate teacher training in the following areas:

Physics
Mathematics
Chemistry
Biology
Balanced Science
Technology
Craft Design and Technology*
Modern Languages
Welsh

* £200 equipment allowance also given with first payment

The bursary is given only to students on a one or two-year Postgraduate Certificate in Education (PGCE) course at a college covered by the scheme, and only to those planning to teach secondary-school-age pupils. It is not available to first degree students. Students on part-time courses receive the bursary on a pro-rata basis. It is not means-tested, and there is no need for you to fill in forms or contact the DFE yourself. Your college will do this for you and the money will be sent to you through them.

The amount being given to students is substantially less than a couple of years ago. This is because more graduates are deciding to take up teaching, but the 'pot of gold' to be shared out is still the same.

To find out more about teaching as a career, contact:
Information Office, TASC, Sanctuary Buildings, Great Smith Street, London SW1P 3BT. Tel: 071-925 5882

To find out more about bursaries, contact:
Department For Education, ITT Bursary Scheme, Mowden Hall, Staindrop Road, Darlington DL3 9BG

TOP UP FUNDS

What is a Postgraduate Experience Allowance?

If you have worked for two years full-time in a job directly relevant to your first degree or proposed course and this includes at least one year since graduating you may qualify for a special allowance which in 1993–4 was:

Age	p.a.
22 years	£ 595
23 years	£1,040
24 years	£1,240
25 years	£1,485
26 years	£1,700
27 years or over	£1,925

What is an Older Student's Allowance?

If you have worked for two years but don't qualify for a postgraduate experience allowance, you might get an older student's allowance. These are slightly less than the rates quoted for postgraduate experience, but well worth claiming (see page 38).

I have three kids and a husband to support – what help is there for me?

If you have been awarded a studentship or bursary and have a family to support then help is at hand. Rates for dependants are generally the same for all awarding bodies give or take a few pounds. In 1994 they were as follows:

	p.a.
Spouse or adult	£1,820
Children under 11	£ 385
aged 11–15	£ 765
aged 16–17	£1,010
aged 18 or over	£1,460

For a single parent £1,820 is allowed for the first child and they can also claim an additional £1,895 if they can demonstrate hardship.

If you have to go away to study and so are keeping two homes you could also claim £635 housing maintenance.

I am disabled – can I get extra help?

Up to £1,140 a year may be paid to students whose disability means additional daily expense. Up to £4,550 for non-medical helpers. Up to £3,415 for specialist equipment.

QUICK CHECK

Awards	In London	Elsewhere	Living at home
BBSRC	£7,950	£6,200	N/A
ESRC	£6,115	£4,720	N/A
MRC	£8,165	£6,145	N/A
NERC	£6,310	£4,950	N/A
EPSRC	£6,115	£4,720	N/A
PPARC	£6,115	£4,720	N/A
BA	£6,115	£4,720	N/A
CCETSW*	£3,098	£2,428	£1,818
MAFF	£6,900	£5,500	N/A
HO* Probation	£3,098	£2,428	£1,818
DFE*	£5,340	£4,245	£3,130
DFE* Bursaries	£3,170	£2,500	£1,890
PGCE*	£2,560	£2,040	£1,615

Plus £1,000 for specific shortage subjects

* = means tested

Are funding arrangements the same for all parts of the UK?

No. For residents in Scotland, Northern Ireland, the Channel Islands and the Isle of Man, funding arrangements are slightly different.

Scotland: Graduates seeking funding for science based subjects are eligible for studentship awards from most of the Research Councils mentioned here. For studentships and bursaries for the arts/ humanities and postgraduate vocational training you should apply to the Scottish Office Education Department (SOED).

Northern Ireland: Funding is provided by three separate bodies.
1. The Department of Agriculture for Northern Ireland (DANI) for study in agriculture, horticulture and related sciences (closing date 28th Feb);
2. The Medical Research council (see details for the UK);
3. The Department of Education for Northern Ireland (DENI), which provides studentships on a competitive basis for courses in humanities, science, technology, social sciences and natural environment studies. Application is through the department where you wish to study. Forms are available in March to be completed by May 1st. DENI also provides bursaries for approved diploma and vocational courses.

Booklet on awards available from the Department of Education for Northern Ireland.

Channel Islands/Isle of Man: apply direct to appropriate education department.

I want to study for the law – what help is there?

With course fees for the Common Professional Examination (CPE), the Postgraduate Diploma in Law and the Legal Practice Course (LPC) running at an average of £4,450, and substantially more at top schools, most students are going to need some help.

1. Sponsorship leading to Articles This is financially the best route. A firm providing sponsorship would pay for your fees at law school for the one or two years, give a maintenance allowance and possibly vacation work. But sponsorship is increasingly competitive and even the very best students are finding it difficult to get. With the recession, firms are cutting back on staff, so there are more good people around to choose from, and less need to secure future staff early. Those who do secure sponsorship would normally expect to serve their articles with that firm. Occasionally a longer commitment to employment is demanded.

2. Summer Placement Programmes A number of firms run Summer Placement Programmes for second-year undergraduates when they will size you up for sponsorship. To get accepted for a course is in itself an achievement, but it is certainly no guarantee of success. The law firm, Clifford Chance, recruits about 90 graduates a year, but only about 20–25 of them are selected from its vacation scheme.

> *'Vacation schemes are . . . an excellent experience, but not an automatic ticket to a training contract if the firm's selection process is exhaustive.'*
> Chris Perrin, Partner, Clifford Chance.

3. Law Society Bursary Scheme Available for students taking CPE and LPC, it is very limited, competitive and includes hardship criteria but worth trying. The bursary is made up from a variety of funds and grant-making trusts which have been grouped together under an umbrella scheme.
Contact: Articles & Admissions Unit, The Law Society, Ipsley Court, Berrington Close, Redditch, Worcestershire B98 0TD.
Tel: 071 242 1222

4. Local Authority Grants Local Authorities are not obliged to fund CPE or LPC students, and rarely do. But they do have discretionary funds available for a wide range of courses and, providing you meet their criteria for awards, you could strike lucky. There are no hard and fast rules, as every local authority has its own. Your local authority may well issue a leaflet giving information on study areas eligible for financial support. Enquire at your local education authority. Failing that contact the Law Society.

5. Ethnic Minority Scholarships A limited number of scholarships are available, mainly for the Legal Practice Course, for ethnic minority students who are British Citizens and want to qualify as solicitors.
Contact: Jerry Garvey, Ethnic Minorities Careers Officer, 50–52 Chancery Lane, London WC2A 1SX.

6. Loans If all other lines of attack have failed there is always a LOAN (see page 152).

Warning note: If you haven't already got articles, getting through law school isn't necessarily a passport to a position in a law firm, not in the

---

CASH CRISIS NOTE:
Some Legal Practice Course Institutions will accept payment of fees by instalments. And part-time study is available throughout the training scheme, including good correspondence courses.

current climate. Abbey, a law graduate studying at one of the top London law schools sent out 300 applications, before getting a job. This is not unusual.

What about other professional qualifications?

Accountants, engineers, actuaries – usually join firms who specialize in that kind of work and they pay for your training and pay you while you are being trained.

OK, so nobody is going to fund me – can I get a loan?

Yes. There are four excellent schemes.

1. **THE CAREER DEVELOPMENT LOAN**

   Available only to those taking a vocational training of up to two years. You can borrow up to £8,000 and not less than £200. The loan is designed to cover course fees (only 80% given if you are in full employment) plus books, materials and living expenses where applicable. The loan is provided by the banks (Barclays, Co-operative, Clydesdale). Interest on the loan is paid by the Government while you are studying and for one month after your course has finished (or up to six months if you are unemployed when repayment should start). If your course costs more than £5,000 or lasts longer than 12 months your local Training and Enterprise Council (TEC) may sponsor you for the additional amount. Check them out. Phone 0800 585 505 for free booklet on Career Development Loans.

2. **THE BUSINESS SCHOOL LOAN SCHEME**

   If you are wanting to take an MBA then the Association of MBAs (AMBA) should be able to help. They run a special scheme to assist graduates and other suitable applicants to study for a master's degree in Business Administration. The scheme is run in conjunction with Barclays and National Westminster banks. To take advantage of the scheme you need to have a bachelor's degree or other suitable professional qualification, a minimum of two years' relevant work experience and to have secured yourself a place on an MBA course at a business school which is on the Association's approved list. Maximum loan for full-time students is two thirds of present or last salary plus tuition fees for each year of study.

Preferential interest rates are given during the course. Repayment starts three months after completion of your course and you have up to seven years to pay it off.

3. LAW SCHOOL LOAN

Assisted by the Law Society, two major banks (National Westminster and Barclays) run a special scheme to help students fund CPE and Legal Practice Courses. The loan, which currently stands at £4,000 p.a. maximum (which isn't enough to cover fees and maintenance), is given at very favourable rates. The Law Society provides application forms for the scheme and when completed these must be returned to the Law Society who will forward them to the bank. To find out more and get an application form, contact: The Law Society, Ipsley Court, Berrington Close, Redditch, Worcestershire B98 0TD. Tel: 071–242 1222 (Ext 3088)

4. POSTGRADUATE LOAN – see chart p. 154

CASH CRISIS NOTE:
If you have just graduated and already have a loan to pay off, think twice before getting even further into debt.

I want to study abroad – can I get help?

Raising finance for postgraduate study abroad is even more difficult, though not completely impossible. Competition is fierce and the opportunities small. The most likely sources are the very limited number of scholarships given to foreign students by the government of host countries or individual institutions. *Study Abroad* published by UNESCO is the best reference source for international scholarships. Otherwise contact the British Council or specific embassies. Many countries produce special literature for foreign students which they will send you. The Commonwealth Scholarship and Fellowship plan is a possible source for those from one commonwealth country visiting another commonwealth country. If you are thinking of the USA then the Fulbright Commission is the best place to start as it administers the annual competition for the Fulbright awards. Leaflets from the Commission covering all aspects of postgraduate study in the USA are available, including details on tuition fees and awards.

WHAT LOANS DO BANKS OFFER TO POSTGRADUATES?

Barclays:

Business School Loan	Two-thirds of salary plus course fees
Law School Loan	£4,000 p.a.
Professional Study Loan (Medicine, Dentistry, Optometry, Veterinary Science)	£3,000 maximum
Career Development Loan (for vocational training lasting at least one week)	£200 minimum; £8,000 maximum

Clydesdale:

Postgraduate Loan (courses at Strathclyde, Stirling & Dundee Universities)	Two-thirds previous salary or £2,000 p.a., plus course fees
Career Development Loan (for vocational training lasting at least one week)	£200 minimum; £8,000 maximum
Professional Studies Loan	Up to £6,000

Co-operative:

Career Development Loan (for vocational training lasting at least one week)	£200 minimum; £8,000 maximum

Lloyds:
Currently reviewing situation

Midland:

Postgraduate Study Loans:	For a 12 month course – £3,000 or two-thirds previous salary + course fees. For a 2 year course – £6,000 or one and one-third previous salary + course fees.

NatWest:
Professional Trainee Loan:

Trainee Barrister	£10,000 over 2 years
Trainee Solicitor	£10,000 over 1 year
Other professions	£5,000 over 1 year
MBA	two-thirds previous salary + course fees.

What help is there for students coming to the UK from abroad?

There are scholarships specifically for overseas students, but these are few, so apply early. The best source for finance is your own home government. Failing that, try the British Government through the British Council, the Foreign and Commonwealth Office or the Overseas Development Agency schemes. There are also the Commonwealth Scholarship Plan, the UN and other international organizations. Some universities give awards and scholarships specially to students from abroad – but each university needs to be contacted individually. Some charitable trusts also cater for foreign students. EGAS (see details on page 128) should be able to help you winkle them out, or check for yourself in appropriate directories (see bibliography below). EC students can compete for UK postgraduate awards already listed in this chapter, but on a fees basis only.

As a student from abroad, what is it really going to cost?

Fees – There is no set rate of fees for postgraduate courses. In the past there has been a recommended minimum but each institution can charge what it wants. Fees for overseas students are generally substantially more than those for home students. EC nationals are generally eligible for home UK student rates. Science courses are usually more expensive than those for the arts.

Recommended minimum for overseas posgraduate fees in 1993/4 were:

Arts:	£5,550
Science:	£7,360
Clinical:	£13,550

Living Expenses – Our survey in Chapter One will give you some idea of what things in Britain are likely to cost. But students with no family close at hand for support are likely to find their needs are more. As a rule of thumb, students from abroad will need £7,000–£10,000 p.a. if studying in London and not less than £5,000 p.a. if studying elsewhere.

Who to contact/What to read:

● *Graduate Studies 1993–4/1994–5*, complete guide to 6,000 postgraduate courses in the UK. CRAC £99.75. Hobsons Publishing

- *Current Research in Britain:* Vol 1–4 covering Physical Sciences, Biological Sciences, Social Sciences, Humanities. Longman

- *British Universities Guide to Graduate Study*, Association of Commonwealth Universities

- *Awards for Postgraduate Study at Commonwealth Universities*, ACU biennial

- *Awards to Women for Graduate Research 1994/95*, British Federation of University Women Graduates, South Bank Business Centre, Park House, 140 Battersea Park Road, London SW11 4NB

- *Postgraduate Study*, Newpoint. Free from Reed Information Services

- *Postgraduate Study and Research*, Graduate Careers Information Booklet – AGCAS The Association of Graduate Careers Advisory Services, CSU (Publications) Ltd, Armstrong House, Oxford Road, Manchester M1 7ED. *Free from your Careers Service.*

- *Postgraduate Management Education*, Graduate Careers Information Booklet – AGCAS The Association of Graduate Careers Advisory Services (as above). *Free from your Careers Service.*

- *POSTGRAD* series covering Engineering, Science, and Information Technology, published by Hobson, Biblios PDF Ltd, Star Road, Partridge Green, West Sussex RH13 8LD or free from your University.

- *PROSPECTS POSTGRAD*, options for further study and research. CSU (Publications) Ltd. Issued once a term.

For Law Students

ROSET (Register of Solicitors Employing Trainees), the most comprehensive information about firms offering sponsorship, available from university or careers services or the Law Society Bookshop, 227/8 The Strand, London WC2A 1BA

PROSPECTS LEGAL, published by the CSU and available from your university or careers service or CSU (Publications) Ltd

The Lawyer Magazine 'Student Special', a supplement published twice a year which lists firms willing to sponsor students. The 'Lawyer' 50 Poland Street, London W1V 4AX. Tel: 071 493 4222

PROSPECTS Legal VacWork, available from your own careers service or CSU (Publications) Ltd.

For Study Abroad

Awards for Postgraduate Study at Commonwealth Universities and *Commonwealth Universities Year-Book*, Association of Commonwealth Universities

Scholarships Abroad, British Council, 65 Davies Street, London W1Y 2AA. Tel: 071-930 8466

Study Abroad, International Scholarships, International Courses – UNESCO, HMSO, PO Box 276, London SW8 5DT

Guide to Awards Open to British Graduate Students For Study in Canada, Canada House, Trafalgar Square, London SW1Y 5BJ

Assistance for Students in Australia and the UK, Australian High Commission, Australia House, London WC2B 4LA

Scholarships and Funding for Study and Research in Germany, German Academic Exchange Service, 17 Bloomsbury Square, London WC1A 2LP

Postgraduate Information Pack, on applying, tuition fees etc. Educational Advisory Service, The Fulbright Commission, Fulbright House, 62 Doughty Street, London WC1N 2LS.

For Foreign Students Studying in the UK

Sources of Financial Assistance for Overseas Students, British Council Publications, available from British Council offices

Studying and Living in Britain, annual handbook, British Council Publications.

7
MAKING THE MONEY GO ROUND

Advice on budgeting

In this final chapter, we try to give you some advice on how to manage your money with the help of Derek Roe, Student Accounts Manager at Midland Bank, who has first hand knowledge of some of the financial difficulties students get themselves into, and how best to help them.

PROBLEMS AND PREDICAMENTS

'My rent is over £30 a week. There's gas and electricity and telephone on top of that, I'm not making ends meet.'

'I've got an overdraft of £700, the bank is charging interest; if I've got an overdraft how can I pay the interest charges?'

'I thought: "£900, wow!" at the beginning of the term and blew the lot in the first few weeks. I haven't even the money for my train fare home.'

'I'm a geography student and have to go on a compulsory trip. Where on earth am I going to find £60?'

'I know now that I shouldn't have bought the car and spent all that money on booze, but . . .'

'Debt – it just crept up on me without my really noticing.'

A BANK MANAGER'S VIEW

'Over £3,000! – It certainly sounds a lot, but is it really? If all you are receiving is the maximum grant, or equivalent from parents, plus maximum loan, then you haven't got wealth beyond the dreams of avarice, but the absolute minimum for survival. Bear that in mind, right from the start and every time temptation looms, then you shouldn't go far wrong. There will always be those who like to live on the edge, spend now and cope with debt and disaster later. Most students who get into debt are genuinely surprised at how easily the money 'just slipped through' their bank account. As the student said, it has a way of just creeping up on you if you let it. So be warned.'

WHAT IS BUDGETING?

The principles are incredibly simple. Putting them into practice is, for many people, incredibly hard. It is a matter of working out what your income and expenses are and making sure the latter doesn't exceed the former. It may sound rather boring, but it's a lot better than being in debt. The students quoted on the previous page obviously didn't budget.

WHERE TO KEEP YOUR MONEY – BANK, BUILDING SOCIETY, UNDER THE MATTRESS, AN OLD SOCK?

Before you can start budgeting you need to choose somewhere to keep your money. We would recommend either a bank or a building society. They are generally quite keen to attract students' accounts because they see students as potential high earners. Earlier in this book there are details of the different freebies the banks offer to entice students to join them. These are worth studying, but shouldn't be the deciding factor. More important is to choose a bank or building society which is located close to your home or place of study. Whilst these days you can use the cash dispensing machines in most branches of most banks and building societies, they haven't yet invented a machine that can give advice.

Counterfoil - not all cheque books have a counterfoil. If yours does always fill it in with the date. Otherwise keep a record of expenditure in the budget pages at the back of your cheque book. It is also a good idea to keep a record in your cheque book of any money you take out of your account through a cash machine.

Date	
Payee	
Balance Bt Fwd	
Other Items	
Total	
£	Balance Cd Fwd

000016

This is the cheque number. Cheques in your book will run consecutively

Write the name of the company or person you are paying the money to.

Write the amount you are paying out here. Write the pounds in words and the pence in figures. Write them closely together leaving no spaces.

THE MONEY BANK
HIGH ST., SOMEWHERE SO1 6XX

Pay

"000016" 64"71-06"   60393 72"

Sorting code – see above.

Your personal account number.

These two dark lines indicate that the cheque is 'crossed'. This means it must be paid into an account.

Write in figures the amount you are paying starting close to the £ sign so no additional figure can be slipped in. Avoid spaces between figures. Always use permanent ink.

This is your branch number. It is printed here to speed up sorting and transferring cheques. It is called the sorting code.

64 - 71 - 06

_____ 19___

or order

£

A. N. OTHER

Insert the date here.

Sign here. When you open your account the bank will ask for a specimen of your signature. Always use the same signature.

N.B. Always write your cheque in ink.

WHAT TYPE OF ACCOUNT?

There are a number of different types of account. At the bank you'll need to open what's called a current account so you can draw money out at any time. Many banks offer accounts specially designed for students, so it's worth checking with them. Some current accounts give interest. It is not as much as a savings account, but every little helps. Check your bank for interest rates.

A building society current account is very similar to a bank account. They too give instant access to your money, and also pay interest on any money in your account. How much depends on the going-rate and your building society.

WHAT WILL YOU GET WHEN YOU OPEN AN ACCOUNT?

When you open an account you may receive a:

- CHEQUE BOOK which you can use to pay big bills and for large purchases.
- CHEQUE GUARANTEE CARD which could be up to £100. This states that the bank will guarantee your cheque up to the amount shown on the card and so the shop where you are making your purchase will let you take the goods away there and then.
- ATM CARD which enables you to withdraw cash from an Automated Teller Machine, and may offer additional payment functions.
- PIN NUMBER – this is your own Personal Identification Number which you will need to remember and use when getting money from the cash dispenser.
- DEBIT CARD (SWITCH OR DELTA) which will automatically debit your account for goods bought when passed through a SWITCH terminal at the point of sale.
- THE THREE-IN-ONE CARD Most banks and building societies combine the facilities mentioned above into multi-functional cards which act as cheque guarantee cards, give access to cash machines and can be used as debit cards so you can purchase goods and services without writing a cheque.
- ACCOUNT NUMBER which you will need for any correspondence with your bank.
- PAYING IN BOOK containing paying-in slips, probably with your branch name printed on them, which you can use when paying in cheques and money. Just fill in the slip and pass it to your bank. Most banks provide

pre-printed envelopes which you can pick up in your branch and then post through a letter box in the banking hall.

- STATEMENT sent to you at regular intervals (we would advise you to ask for it monthly). The statement will give details of the money going in and out of your account – an essential part of budgeting properly.

CAUTION

Don't keep your cheque guarantee card and cheque book together. If stolen, somebody could clean out your account.

Keep your Personal Number (PIN) secret. Never write it down or tell it to anyone else.

Cheques take three days to clear from an account. So don't go on a mad spending spree if you find you have more money in your account than you thought. The read-out on the cash-dispensing machine may not be up-to-date.

YOUR INCOME – HOW MUCH?

It's all very well to have an official piggy bank in which to keep your money, but where is the money going to come from and how much is it likely to be? If you have read the rest of this book, you should by now have some idea how much you are likely to have as a student. If you look at our budgeting plan, we have listed some of the likely sources. With a little ingenuity you may have discovered others.

Now let's get down to it.

HOW TO WORK OUT A SIMPLE BUDGETING PLAN

1 Take a piece of paper and divide into three columns. One the left hand side write down your likely income sources and how much they will provide, i.e.
    - grant
    - parental contribution

- student loan
- money from access fund
- money earned from holiday job
- sponsorship etc.

Now total them up.

The trouble with budgeting, especially for students, is that money generally comes in at one time, often in large chunks at the beginning of a term, and your outgoings at another. When you work you will probably find it easiest to budget on a monthly basis, but as a student you will probably have to do it either termly or yearly depending on how the money comes in.

2 In the middle column write down your fixed expenses – things that you have to pay out like rent, gas, electricity, telephone, food etc. Don't forget to include fares. Now total them up.

INCOME		OUTGOINGS		
		Predicted		*Actual*
Grant	£	Rent/College Board	£	£
Parental Contrib.	£	Gas	£	£
Student Loan	£	Electricity	£	£
Sponsorship	£	Telephone	£	£
Holiday Job	£	Launderette/cleaning	£	£
Access Fund	£	Food	£	£
		Fares while in college	£	£
		Fares to college	£	£
		Car expenses	£	£
		Books/Equipment	£	£
		Compulsory trips	£	£
		TV licence	£	£
		Student rail/bus card	£	£
Total:	£	**Total:**	£	
		Socialising	£	£
		Hobbies	£	£
		Entertainment	£	£
		Clothes	£	£
		Presents	£	£
		Holidays	£	£

3 Subtract your fixed expenses from your income and you will see just how much you have, or haven't, got left over to spend.

Draw a line under the list in your right hand column and now list your incidental expenses, things like socialising, clothes, the cinema, hobbies, birthdays, etc. This is your 'do without column': the area where you can juggle your expenses to make ends meet.

4 Apportion what's left over to the things listed in this final column making sure you've got at least something left over for emergencies. Do the figures add up?

Seems simple enough and logical on paper. But of course it doesn't work quite as easily as that. There's always the unexpected. You can't get a job. Your car needs a new battery. People use more gas than expected. Did I really talk for that long on the phone?

5 Having worked out your budget, use the final column on your budget sheet to fill in exactly how much your bills do come to. In this way you can keep a check on your outgoings and how accurate your predictions were, and do something BEFORE the money runs out.

A BANK MANAGER'S VIEW

'It's all very well for the prudent bank manager to say work out your budget, but how does a pre-university student do this for a place where they've never lived before. The answer is to visit the town where you intend to study, and organize your accommodation as soon as possible. Accommodation will be your biggest single outgoing. If you are not staying in halls of residence you'll probably find that accommodation close to the campus goes early, and so then you would have incidentals like bus fares and taxis to consider – they can soon mount up. The cost of accommodation can vary. What you would get for £35 in Durham may cost you £45 in Brighton.'

WHAT IS A STANDING ORDER?

Regular payments such as rent can be paid automatically by the bank through a standing order. You just tell the bank how much to pay out and to whom and they will do the rest. The system is ideal for people who are bad at getting round to paying their bills. Forget to pay the electricity and you'll soon know. Standing orders are not so easy to organize when you are in shared accommodation with everyone chipping in on the bill.

WHAT IS A DIRECT DEBIT?

With a direct debit again the bill is paid automatically, but it works in a different way. The bank of the organization you are paying the money to will collect the money direct from your account. This is an ideal way of paying when the amount being paid out is likely to change.

CARDS AND THE CATCHES

Credit Cards: These are an easy way to pay for things but can also be an easy way to get into debt. When you have a card such as Access, Visa or Barclaycard, you are given a credit limit. This means you can make purchases up to that sum. Each month you receive a statement of how much you owe. If you pay back the whole lot immediately there are no interest charges. If you don't, you will pay interest on the balance. There is an annual charge for credit cards. You can use your card in the UK and abroad at most shops and many restaurants. They are a way of getting short-term credit but are an expensive way of borrowing long-term.

Store Cards: Many stores such as Marks and Spencer offer credit cards which operate in much the same way as described above, but can only be used in that particular store or chain of stores. Cards are too easy to come by. Get a stack of them and you could find you're 'seriously' in debt.

Debit Cards: You've probably seen the SWITCH card in action as many stores and garages now have the SWITCH system installed: look for the green SWITCH logo. By simply passing your debit card through a SWITCH terminal, the price of the purchase you are making is automatically deducted from your account. What could be easier? Details of the transaction will show up on your next statement.

SAFETY CHECK: most banks and building societies will NOT send plastic cards or pin numbers to customers living in halls of residence or multi-occupancy lodging, because they could go astray or sit in the hall way for days unclaimed. All too easy to steal.

CAUTION

Look carefully at any interest being charged and for hidden costs.

WHAT IF THE MONEY RUNS OUT?

Help, I am in debt!

Don't panic, but don't sweep the matter under the carpet and try to ignore it because it won't go away. In fact it will just get worse. Get in touch with your Student Welfare Officer at your university, or the student adviser at your local university branch, or your bank manager. Or all three. Through experience they will be able to give the best advice and help. Impoverished and imprudent students are not a new phenomenon.

Getting an Overdraft

You don't get 'owt' for 'nowt' – well rarely. Most banks are fairly generous to students and do allow them to be overdrawn sometimes without charging. If you look back in this book at the section on *What the Banks Offer* (pp. 62–3), you'll see they do offer free overdraft facilities to students up to around £400. Some banks offer this facility for the full duration of your course; others stipulate just the first year. BUT DON'T TAKE IT AS RIGHT. Always ask your Bank first if they will grant you this facility. Otherwise you will be in trouble and could be charged. And remember whatever you borrow eventually has to be paid back.

If you find yourself overdrawn, get on the phone or call in immediately to your bank. Many of the clearing banks have campus branches or at least a branch in the town geared to dealing with students. They'll probably be sympathetic and come up with a helpful solution.

Borrowing on credit

'Haven't got the money at the moment so I'll buy it on Access.'

Easily done, but be warned, though Access/Visa is excellent as a payment card, credit can cause problems. If you don't pay off your bill at the end of the month, you will have to pay interest and, compared with other sources of borrowing, this is very high. Unlike your friendly bank, credit card companies are not the sort of people you can negotiate with, and are very likely to sue. Don't see them as another source of income.

A planned overdraft

'I'm going for an interview and need something to wear.'

This is not an unusual request from students in their final year. Banks are very good at coming up with a plan to help you out with an obvious or specific need. After all, an interview success could mean you'll clear your overdraft that much quicker.

An overdraft is often the cheapest way of borrowing, but there are charges and interest rates, which need to be checked out. The advantage of an overdraft is that you don't have to pay it back in fixed amounts, though the bank has the right to ask for its money back at any time.

Personal Loans

This is quite different from an overdraft. It is usually used when you want to borrow a much larger sum, over a longer period – say several years. It differs from an overdraft in that you borrow an agreed amount over a set period of time and the repayments are a fixed amount, generally monthly. You might take out a loan to pay for your course fees but not for short-term credit to tide you over until your next grant cheque arrives.

CAUTION

Don't borrow from a lot of places. If you've got an overdraft and a Student Loan, that's probably enough.

How the Bank Manager can help

Don't be afraid to go into your bank and ask for help. Most banks have specially trained student advisers on the premises, to help students like you. They will arrange bank accounts, discuss overdrafts, help with budgeting. It's what they've been trained for. Many of them have recently been students, so they know the ropes, and the difficulties.

DEALING WITH DEBT

Tanya's Story
I made a real mess of my finances in my first year. Spend, spend, spend. The result – the confiscation of my cash-point and cheque cards and the need to borrow money from my mother in order to placate an angry bank manager.

As I find it very difficult to restrain myself financially, I devised a plan to prevent myself getting into such a situation again. I organized my money into two bank accounts: one for general living expenses such as food, going out, clothes; the other for bills and running expenses on my car. I then sat down and worked out how best to divide my money between these two accounts. So, I now have a weekly sum which goes into the food account, for which I now have a cash-card, and a monthly sum which goes into the other account. For this I have a cheque book, but no card.

This way, if I err, then I only go hungry on the last couple of days of the week and there is always money enough to pay the bills. If you suffer from the same weakness as me, ask your bank manager to organize a similar solution for you. I can recommend the peace of mind, even though it's occasionally on an empty stomach.

DON'TS

(which unfortunately some students do)

● don't fall into the hands of a loan shark. Any loan offered to students, except from a recognised student source, i.e. the banks, building societies, parents or the student loan scheme, should be treated with the utmost caution and suspicion. It's bound to cost you an arm and a leg, and lead to trouble.

- don't run up an overdraft with your bank without asking first – even the much vaunted interest free overdraft offered by most banks to students should be checked out first, otherwise you might find you are being charged. They need to know you are a student.

- don't forget to pay your gas and electricity bills. Make them top priority. A week or two on bread and jam is better than having to pay court costs.

- don't pawn your guitar, only to find you can't afford to get it out to play at the next gig.

- don't try 'kiting'. The banks have got wind of what's been going on, and you're bound to be found out and in real trouble. For the uninitiated like this author, *kiting* is the dishonest practice of making the most of the time lapse between people reporting that their credit card is missing, and it being recorded as stolen. It works like this, and only on a Saturday: you give your cheque card to a friend to buy all your favourite videos, CDs, food for the weekend or whatever. He, or possibly she, then whips in and out of the shop and makes the grand purchase while you make the phone call reporting that the card is lost. You then presumably share the spoils. Be warned, it is a criminal offence, and could end up increasing your debts – or even worse.

- don't get black listed with the bank. 'Kiting' is a sure way of getting a bad record. Running up an overdraft is another.

- don't see credit cards as another source of income.

SAVINGS?

Most books on budgeting give lengthy advice on saving. We think it unlikely that students will do more than just make ends meet and even that will be a struggle. However, if you do find that you have some surplus cash, or have taken out the Student Loan as an investment (see page 49), then it would be advisable to open a savings account at a bank, a building society or the Post Office. Check out the interest rates and the terms and conditions. Many high-interest accounts give limited access to your money – so, watch out.

A BANK MANAGER'S VIEW

'The problems students have are very real. As a bank manager, all too often we find we are just picking up the pieces when things have gone too far. Debt brings stress, and that will affect your ability to study. Come sooner rather than later.'

We thought we'd let a student have the final word:

'Before they start a degree students don't realise just how tough it's going to be. You think, how on earth can anybody be so irresponsible as to get £3,000 worth of debt? But once you are into university life, you know only too well. Despite the hardship, don't be put off, University is excellent – an incredible experience not to be missed!'
Andrea, reading Law at Brunel University – expects to graduate with £3,000 of debt.

Best of luck . . .

Index

Other essential books from Trotman's...

The Complete Degree Course Offers 1995
by Brian Heap
25th Edition
This essential book for applicants to higher education includes points
requirements for entry to all first degree courses, advice on how to choose
a course and institution, information on how to complete the new section
10 on the UCAS form and much more.
Price: £14.95
Published April 1994

How To Choose Your Degree Course
by Brian Heap
4th Edition
The long awaited new edition of this book contains general advice on how
to go about choosing which degree subject to study, looking at A-level
subjects and their related courses, and at career groups and specific
careers.
Price: £11.95
Published April 1994

How To Choose Your Higher National Diploma Course
Second Edition
This extensively revised and updated publication provides information on:
entrance requirements, course descriptions, selection criteria and
procedures, intake numbers and applications received, sponsorship and
work placements, employment statistics as well as information on GNVQs
and NVQs.
Price: £14.95
Published December 1993

Order Form (please photocopy)

Please send me the following books:

		Qty	Total
Degree Course Offers 1995	£14.95 + 2.20 p+p	_____	£_____
How To Choose Your Degree Course	£11.95 + 2.20 p+p	_____	£_____
How To Choose Your HND Course	£14.95 + 2.20 p+p	_____	£_____
		Total	**£_____**

*Please call us on 081-332-2132 for Access and Visa orders and postage and packing
rates for multiple copy orders.*

Trotman books are available through good bookshops everywhere.

Cash Orders: Please make your cheque payable to **Trotman & Company** and send it to:
12 Hill Rise, Richmond, Surrey, TW10 6UA.
Credit Orders: only for schools'/organisations' orders of **over £35**. Please attatch your **official order
form** to ours. The original invoice will be sent with the books, payment is due within 28 days.